TRAINING IN
DEPTH INTERVIEWING

P116-117

Under the editorship of Wayne Holtzman

TRAINING IN DEPTH INTERVIEWING

WILLIAM H. BANAKA

UNIVERSITY OF PORTLAND

HARPER & ROW, PUBLISHERS

NEW YORK   EVANSTON   SAN FRANCISCO   LONDON

CONTENTS

PREFACE

Are you looking for ways to make your next interview better? Do you wonder whether you can more quickly diagnose and resolve difficulties you experience with interviewees? Do you wonder whether the cost of interviewing (estimates range from $15 to $100 an hour) is worth it? As a beginner or as an experienced interviewer, if you are asking yourself such questions, you will, I believe, find this book valuable. It is a training aid for people learning how better to conduct the information-gathering interview. It does not go into the parts of counseling or therapeutic interviewing in which attitudinal and/or behavior change is intended. It may be used as a text in a course or workshop aimed at professional training in interviewing of any kind—since information gathering usually is a starting point for the counseling interview.

You may use the book on your own as a self-training device. Depth interviewers in these fields will find the training aids relevant: survey research, employment, placement, rehabilitation, nursing, clinical psychiatry, clinical psychology, dentistry, vocational counseling, social work, legal investigation, forensics, police investigation, credit interviewing, insurance adjustment, organizational research, journalism, and human relations problem-solving in organizations.

What is in the book? First, an interpersonal theory that is

relevant and specific to understanding the interactions in an interview. Second, a series of detailed guides for each step of the interview process: how to plan, how to set up a practice interview, how to summarize obtained data and do a content and process analysis, and how to evaluate your interviewing skills. The interpersonal theory and the specific evaluation of your interview behaviors are interwoven throughout the text. The approach is interactional, stressing your objective analytical and subjective sensitivity skills about yourself, about an interviewee, and about the results of your interactions on each other.

Chapter 1 describes a theory of interpersonal communication I have found most relevant and workable for understanding the subtleties of interviewing. The theory combines ideas from Bill Schutz (1958, 1967), who stresses the affective aspects of human interactions, and from Robert Bales (1950), who studies both the cognitive and affective dimensions of interpersonal behaviors. The theory tells us where to look for significant verbal and nonverbal events in the interview, and what to do to improve the communications.

Chapters 2 and 3 are designed to help you increase your awareness of your own logical and relational (affective) experiences in interactions with others. Special emphasis is placed on your learning to experience your own *feelings*. All persons have rich subjective perceptions; a skilled interviewer is able to integrate his emotional awareness into his interviewing behavior. You can do some of the exercises in Chapter 2 by yourself. Other parts of Chapter 2, and the interviewer role-plays in Chapter 3, require a partner. If you are a beginner, or if you have never had prior training experience in dealing with verbal and nonverbal expressions of feelings, these two chapters are especially important. Chapter 3 also suggests specific ways to observe for nonverbal cues about feelings and to evaluate the directness or indirectness of how feelings are communicated. Ways to evaluate the logical skills of an interviewer also are suggested.

Chapter 4 shifts to the planning process for an interview.

Before doing an interview, do you stop to think about what you will *do* with whatever information you get? That's called the OUTPUT. The output may be decisions about the interviewee or analyses or predictions about how he might do if selected for a certain position or assigned to a particular type of therapy. If this decision theory mode of thinking is novel to you, Chapter 4 is important.

Chapter 5 is for the inexperienced interviewer. It describes how to make the specific arrangements for a practice interview.

Chapter 6 provides a method for evaluating data obtained from the interviewee. The method is called analysis of the manifest content. You determine how much of the planned input you actually got and how well documented your output conclusions may be. This gives you a surface picture of verbal events in the interview—a thorough, line-by-line summary of what you actually did in terms of language content from the interviewee. This training, incidentally, is also relevant to content analysis in any type of research.

Chapter 7 outlines a way to categorize interviewer and interviewee inputs so you will know exactly what types of questions you asked and what types of answers you got. In effect, the thematic analysis of Chapter 6 is broken down into levels of communication within the thematic content.

Chapters 8 and 9 describe how to critique an interview in more detail and relate your interview experience to the theory discussed in Chapter 1. A method for critiquing some of the crucial interactions in terms of the interpersonal theory—how you and the interviewee were reacting to the logical and relational issues as they occurred—is presented in Chapter 8. This analysis of critical interactions is best done after you have categorized the inputs of the interview.

In Chapter 9, other ways to analyze the interview and sum up your strengths and weaknesses are suggested. Because much emphasis is placed on nonverbal data, Chapter 9 is especially useful if you have video equipment. But it is a good idea to pull together your observations about how you did on both the intellectual and emotional and the verbal and at least the audible nonverbal dimensions of the interview, if you have only audio equipment. If you have neither audio nor video equipment, you will not be able to do what is suggested in chapters 6 through 9.

What about the theoretical, practical, and research literature? The text is kept as brief as possible to facilitate your understanding of the multitude of factors involved in interviewing. Important ideas and research findings are detailed in the Annotated Bibliography at the back of the book. The theories and practical guides cited there are, in my judgment, in keeping with the training goals of this book. Research approaches and findings that add to our knowledge of dyadic behavior and the setting in which it occurs also are called to your attention.

Many of the ideas about evaluating the interview came from Ronald Wilson while I was a graduate student at the University of Houston. John Wallen has helped me see how Bales' and Schutz' theories connect and apply. More credit is due the numerous undergraduate and graduate students who have struggled and grown with me in courses on interviewing at the University of Portland. In 1969, Jack Scranton was especially helpful in editing portions of the book and helping adapt to the (then) new challenge of using video equipment.

I am indebted most of all to my wife, Helen, who not only fully supported my efforts to write this book but often shows me how to freshen and sharpen our own efforts to communicate!

TRAINING IN
DEPTH INTERVIEWING

1

THE COMMUNICATION PROCESS IN A DEPTH INTERVIEW

What makes a good depth interview? What knowledge and skills does a good interviewer have? What affects the quality of interviewee responses? Do the same interviewing techniques work equally well with all types of interviewee personalities? How deep into his own personality must a trainee interviewer go to develop good interviewing skills?

A good depth interview results from the interviewer's knowing and using a workable theory of interpersonal communication. Less important is his knowing the standard prescriptions for techniques of interviewing. If you are aware of the key objective and subjective factors that influence how two people relate to each other, you can facilitate the communication well enough to accomplish the purpose of the interview. Hence, the emphasis in this book is on understanding and applying a theory of interpersonal communication to the interviewing process.

THE FOCUS IS ON *YOU*

You are challenged to understand the theory by learning about yourself. You are challenged to look deeply into your own ways of reacting—inwardly first, then outwardly. You are to learn how to use your own thinking and feelings to further the communications process. How does this book help you do that? This chapter explains the theory. Chapter 2 puts *you* in the picture—letting you experience what the theory is about.

DEFINITION OF DEPTH INTERVIEWING

What is a depth interview? What kinds of interpersonal communications are involved in interviewing? There are three phases in depth interviewing: input, analysis, and output. *Input* refers to the information obtained from EE,* ER's questions, and EE's answers; *analysis* refers to the inferences made by ER about EE's input and behavior during the interview; and *output* refers to the conclusions ER makes at the end of his analysis. Output conclusions are diagnoses of causes of EE's problem, predictions about how EE will behave in future situations, and decisions about what should be done to help EE with his problem. Putting these three phases together, we define a depth interview as

> the gathering of a sufficient amount and kind of information (INPUT), for thorough analysis (ANALYSIS), in order to make accurate decisions about EE's behavior under certain conditions (OUTPUT).

A radio announcer interviewing the man-on-the-street is not participating in a depth interview. He is conducting only the input phase, asking for EE's personal opinions and feelings on a specific topic, in order to keep the attention of his listening audience.

The theory in this chapter will help you to do the analysis and show you how to get sufficient input from EE so that your output conclusions will be accurate. Now, let us see how we can analyze interpersonal communications.

INTERPERSONAL COMMUNICATIONS

THEORY TELLS US WHERE TO LOOK

How can we go about understanding what happens in interpersonal communications? There are literally hundreds of events

* Throughout the text we shall use the abbreviations EE for "interviewee" and ER for "interviewer."

every few seconds. Some events are verbal—what is being said. Some events are nonverbal—facial expressions, body movements, tone of voice, laughing, sighing. A useful theory will tell us which of all these events provide pertinent information. Our theory has two vantage points: the manifest content and the interpersonal processes. The manifest content, what is said in an interview, is available from a transcript or tape. The interpersonal processes are the underlying thoughts and feelings the persons are having as they are communicating. Let us see how we can use each vantage point.

THE MANIFEST CONTENT —substance

The manifest content are the words spoken in the interview. You analyze it by sorting EE responses into topics and then summarizing what you obtained from him. The analysis shows you what topics were well covered, what topics were only partially covered, and what topics were omitted. It is adequacy of coverage you are interested in in evaluating manifest content. Chapter 6 shows how to do a manifest content analysis.

THE INTERPERSONAL PROCESSES

The underlying dynamics of the interpersonal processes may be broken down into two dimensions: the logical, for the thinking process, and the relational, for the feeling process. You will find the identification and analysis of the logical and relational interpersonal processes more difficult than the analysis of manifest content. Your private thoughts and feelings are only partly revealed in your overt behavior. As you increase your awareness of your private world of feelings, you will sense more your part of the interpersonal dynamics. As for EE, however, you will have to infer how he is thinking and feeling. The rest of this chapter explains three types of logical issues and three types of relational issues. You will see how they are defined, how they show up in interactions, and how to deal with them effectively.

THE LOGICAL ISSUES

The logical process is the way ER and EE appear to think as an interview proceeds. How ER and EE appear to think shows up in the continuity or discontinuity of communication levels. The continuity of the logical process may be analyzed by the ways ER and EE respond to these three logical issues.

Information. What data are needed? How are terms defined?
Opinion. What are our goals? What is causing the problem? How well will your proposed solution work?
Action. What are we going to do?

What are the earmarks of effective logical communication?

1. The two persons stay on the same topic.
2. Each person is willing to share his relevant information, opinions, and ideas about action.
3. Each person is willing to stay at the same logical level until both are satisfied they are ready to go to the next relevant logical level.
4. Each person is willing to shift from one logical level to the prior logical level when progress is blocked. Information is logically prior to opinion; opinion is prior to action; and action is prior to information.

How do people typically handle the logical levels of communication? When you observe two people or a group of people discussing a problem, you may notice that the progress is almost random, disorderly. Participants in a problem-solving discussion act as if they are unaware of the different logical levels of communication; if somewhat aware, they find it difficult to influence the other person to make the discussion more logical. Here is an example which illustrates ineffective logical communication.

Input	*Analysis*
1. JOHN: Let's go to the beach, Mary.	John proposes action.
2. MARY: No, it will probably rain there today.	Mary shifts the level to an opinion about the weather.
3. JOHN: But the weather	John tries to "reason" with

forecast is for clear skies there.	Mary by shifting to information about the weather forecast.
4. MARY: You know the forecast is often wrong.	Mary disputes John's information by expressing an opinion.

This discontinuous conversation goes from action to opinion, then to information, next to opinion. No issue is resolved before the next issue is raised. How might John resolve the first action issue he raised? Perhaps in this way:

Input	*Analysis*
5. JOHN: Mary, it sounds like you just aren't interested in going to the beach. Is that true?	John asks Mary to give him a direct answer to the action issue he raised in input 1 above.
6. MARY: You're right. I really don't feel like going to the beach.	Mary gives John the direct answer, apart from other issues.
7. JOHN: Why is that?	John shifts to the logically prior level, asking Mary to explain her reasons for not wanting to go.
8. MARY: We've had such bad luck with the weather when we've gone this year, I feel queasy about trying it again. Besides, it's a lot of work to get everything ready.	Mary responds to John's shift to the opinion level, giving "bad luck," "feel queasy," and "lot of work" as her reasons.
9. JOHN: I was so excited about going, I guess I was willing to take the risk with the weather. But I sure see why you don't feel like trying it.	John stays at the same opinion level, sharing his own opinions and showing he accepts Mary's opinions and feelings.

10. MARY: Thanks. *(Smiles)* — Mary shows appreciation and relief. The prior opinion issue has been clarified.

11. JOHN: What would you like to do today? — John shifts back to action, now that the logically prior issue has been cleared.

12. MARY: I feel more like working in the garden today. — Mary again cooperates by directly answering John's action question.

13. JOHN: Okay. It's more important for me to spend the day with you than to go to the beach. I'll work with you in the garden. — John now is able to decide on his preference for action.

The analysis shows how to resolve an action issue by shifting to the logically prior opinion (and feeling) issues. If John had felt stronger about going to the beach, he might have further pursued Mary's opinion about "bad luck with the weather" by shifting to informational issues. In this example, he is satisfied by Mary's several direct answers (inputs 6, 8, and 12). This example illustrates the four earmarks of effective logical communication.

How are logical issues identified? First you look at what is said, and then you align that content with the apparent logical level. A logical issue may be inferred in every verbalization. As you become more aware of the logical level of each ER and EE input,* you then will be able to recognize the signals of discontinuous communication. In turn, recognition of a signal also tells you what, logically, to do to restore continuity. Each signal is the obverse of the four earmarks of effective logical communication. Here is a summary of the signals of discontinuous communication and ways to restore continuity.

* You will get practice in identifying logical issues in the next two chapters. And in Chapter 8, you will learn how to evaluate your handling of logical issues in a practice interview.

Logical issue	Resolution
1. ER or EE suddenly changes the topic before finishing the previous one.	ER returns to the unfinished topic as soon as possible. If EE persists in changing the topic, ER confronts him about that behavior.
2. EE appears unwilling to continue giving information on a topic.	ER asks EE if he is unwilling to continue. ER then tries to help EE deal with the reasons for his unwillingness.
3. ER or EE shifts the logical level before enough closure is obtained.	ER recognizes a priority of logical issues. If action issues cannot be resolved, he next asks EE about his opinions (goals, predictions, analysis of causes). If an opinion issue cannot be resolved, ER goes to the information level to get more facts or to clarify EE's definition of terms. ER keeps structuring the level of communication until the logically prior issue is identified and resolved.
4. ER or EE refuses to cooperate in shifting to logically prior issues.	ER asks EE the reasons for his refusal to give opinions or factual information. EE's or ER's feelings about their relationship may be a contributing factor.

Each of these suggestions involves you, as ER, giving EE feedback about the logical process going on, as you see it. At first, this confrontational feedback process may seem awkward—or even threatening—to you, because it is not usually done in interpersonal relations. Such feedback is vital to effective communications. As you gain confidence in diagnosing the logical issues, monitoring your own discontinuities and confronting EE about his discontinuities will be much easier.

A special burden to ER is that he must watch for both his and EE's reactions to logical issues. Inexperienced ERs tend to make more logical blunders than the volunteer EEs they are interviewing. Practice will help you become aware of your style of dealing with logical issues.

Especially helpful in resolving logical issues is the fact that they have a priority, as indicated in the resolution of the third discontinuity in the preceding table. Disagreement on the level of action can be resolved by moving to the level of opinions about past experience, about goals or relative merits of different action alternatives. Disagreement about the relative merits of different action alternatives can be resolved by moving to the prior issue of information and definitions of terms. Opinions about the merits of an action alternative are based on one's understanding of his data on circumstances and present situational conditions. If enough data about the past and present are shared, the advantages and disadvantages of each action alternative will be clearer to the discussants. Thus, the priorities of logical issues go from action to opinion to information. When stuck at one level, go to the prior level.

An informational base is vital to the flow of discussion at the other two levels of logical communication. A skillful ER always begins by asking EE for a word picture of his past experiences that are related to the topic of the interview. This informational base enables ER to probe later for EE's opinions and feelings about his past experience, his present circumstances, and future plans. It also gives EE confidence that ER understands the realities he has experienced. Chapters 3 and 5 give further details on how to begin the interview.

What if EE simply refuses, after ER has provided adequate feedback, to give some kinds of information? As indicated in the resolution of the fourth discontinuity, part of the reason may be a relational issue between ER and EE. The occurrence of such an issue indicates a problem in trust between ER and EE; it is at the heart of the challenge to ER. Ways for dealing with them are explained in the following section.

THE RELATIONAL ISSUES

Logical and relational issues occur concomitantly in an interpersonal communication. The three relational issues (from Schutz, 1967) are reflected in the way each communicant feels about himself and the other person.

Inclusion. Am I "in" or "out" of the relationship? How committed am I?

Control. How much influence do I wield in the relationship? Am I "on top" or "on bottom"?

Affection. How do I feel—love, indifference, hate—about the other person? Do I want to be closer to or further away from him? Do I want to hug him, ignore him, or hit him?

Any of the three may surface at any time in an interpersonal communication. The INCLUSION issue arises especially as a new relationship is being formed. It also is an issue whenever a new task or purpose is proposed in an on-going relationship. Each person has to find his degree of involvement in, and commitment to, the proposed action, be it an interview or a trip to the beach. Inclusion issues are unresolved when one person is unable to participate freely in the proposed action.

The perceived distribution of power or influence in a relationship is the basis for the CONTROL issue. Once an interaction has begun, the selection of topic, the choice of level of logical communication, and the norms for verbal and nonverbal behavior are worked out by the two people. A control issue arises if at any choice point, one person perceives that he is unduly or inappropriately dominated by the other.

The AFFECTION issue refers to the feeling tone one person has for another. In a new relationship, the initial impulse may be to like or dislike the other person. As a relationship develops, each usually experiences a range of positive and negative feelings about the other person. An initial "like," for example, may be dampened if one learns that the other is diametrically opposed to his opinion on an important matter. An initially unfavorable impression may be changed when one finds that he and the other share a strong interest in some activity. In the interview, ER's opinions and feelings are more affected by negative and contradictory data from EE (Bolster and Springbett, 1961*).

What are the earmarks of effective relational communication?

1. Each person is willing to share his feelings about the relationship.
2. Each person expresses his feelings directly, not indirectly. For example, if ER is tense and nervous when starting an interview, he shares these feelings with EE. An indirect expression of a feeling puts the locus of the experience outside the speaker—for example, if a student tries to play a role and "flops," he may say: "Well, it was an artificial situation; that's not what I'm *really* like." Direct expression means that the person "owns" his feelings, is nondefensive, and exposes his feelings when they are relevant.
3. Each person is aware of and acknowledges his nonverbal as well as his verbal expression of feelings. This dimension relates to magnitude—how intensively and with how wide a variety of nonverbal behaviors a person communicates—and to directness versus indirectness.
4. Verbalized feelings and nonverbal behavior are congruent. ER asks EE: "Are you tense?" EE replies, with a stiffened posture and wrinkled forehead: "Oh, no. I'm not tense." Here nonverbal and verbal behavior contradict each other.
5. Each person shows concern and acceptance for the other person's feelings. A person asks what another is experiencing when he sees cues of a strong feeling; he is nonjudgmental when the other person does expose a feeling; and he shares his own feelings, when relevant. For example, when EE has exposed a strong feeling of fear, ER may reciprocate by stating: "I have been afraid in similar situations." Or, if ER is confused or out of touch, he admits it: "I know

---

* See Annotated Bibliography, p. 184.

you feel strongly, but I'm not quite with you. Tell me more." The point here is that exposing a deep feeling often leaves a person feeling "out on a limb." ER should reassure EE by responding with equal depth of feeling—but, of course, ER should not shift the focus from EE to himself.

6. Willingness to persist in the exploration of relational feelings so that the tension created by an affection issue can be reduced and effective logical discussion continued.

What are the earmarks of ineffective relational communication? One or both persons are unaware, unable, or unwilling to pursue their feelings. Let us return to John and Mary. Suppose John had not tried to resolve the action issue:

JOHN: Let's go to the beach, Mary.
MARY: No, it will probably rain there today.
JOHN: But the weather forecast is for clear skies there.
MARY: You know the forecast is often wrong.
JOHN: *(Sighs)* Okay, okay. Forget it. *(Walks off, tensely)*

In this example, each is somewhat aware of an uneasiness or tension. John shows it in his nonverbal sigh, and feels unresolved as he leaves. Mary, too, has some degree of awareness that they have failed to relate well. John is avoiding further exposure of his feelings by walking off. Mary is implicitly agreeing not to pursue the relational issues involved by keeping silent as John departs. To be effective, both persons must be able and willing to expose their feelings more directly. How might this happen?

JOHN: *(Returns after a few minutes)* Mary, I really wanted to go to the beach, but you shot me down.
MARY: I know, but it just wouldn't be any fun today.
JOHN: You're always pessimistic. (Relational issue—AFFECTION) I feel sad now. (Relational issue—INCLUSION)
MARY: You're always trying to make me do what I don't want to do. (Relational issue—CONTROL) Why don't you let me decide once in a while? I don't feel like you really let me do what I want to do. It makes me feel cut off. (Relational issue—INCLUSION)

Now John and Mary have both disclosed their feelings about each other. Note that they ranged across the three types of relational issues: affection, inclusion, and control. Once the strong relevant feelings have been disclosed (and often the irrelevant feelings, too), it is possible to resolve the relational and logical issues. Mary might initiate the resolution like this:

MARY: Now I see the problem I made for you. I wasn't reacting to your idea about going to the beach at all. I just didn't want you dominating me again.

JOHN: Yes, I feel that often you aren't even talking about my ideas or suggestions. What can I do to help you feel like you have more of a say-so in our decisions?

MARY: Well, for a start, you could slow down. Give me time to come up with some ideas and suggestions. You overwhelm me by always initiating the discussion about what we're going to do.

JOHN: Okay, I guess I can try that. What will help us work this one out today?

MARY: Just give me a few minutes. Then I'll come up with a suggestion for something interesting for us to do for the day.

JOHN: Okay. Let me know when you're ready.

MARY: I will. And please let me fully explain what my suggestion is before you start talking about it.

JOHN: Okay. Let's try it.

John has agreed to defer his need to enjoy the beach in order to give Mary a chance to feel better about their control process. He can sense that it is unlikely that they will feel positively toward each other until Mary feels more equal to him in their decision-making. This example illustrates the six earmarks of good relational communication.

How are relational issues identified? They are emotional reactions, which are usually not clearly included in verbal communications among adults. The emotional reactions may be detected by watching the nonverbal expressions of each person, either by direct observation or by videotaping. They may be exposed by the direct verbal expression of each person's affective reactions about himself and the other person. Many people in our culture are inhibited about the direct expression of their inner reactions or feelings. Chapters 2 and 3 are designed to help you become more aware of how you experience the relational issues and how you deal with your inner reactions. As you gain more awareness of your inner reactions, and cues about EE's feelings, you will be able to deal with relational issues as they occur.

How are the relational issues resolved? Typically, they do not get resolved: they are avoided. Following are some of the ways of avoiding a relational issue:

1. One or both persons privately discount how they are feeling.
2. One person perceives a nonverbal reaction in the other, assumes he knows enough of how the other person feels, and proceeds without checking out his perception.
3. One person obviously is experiencing an inner reaction, and the other person avoids it with any of a number of rationalizations:
   ☐ "It would embarrass him."
   ☐ "It would make his feelings 'worse' or stronger."
   ☐ "It might hurt him if I give him feedback on how he seems to feel."
   ☐ "It's up to him to expose a feeling if he has one."
4. Sensing some tension between them, one person "inadvertently" changes the topic to reduce the tension.

Relational issues are resolved by direct confrontation when one or both persons believe tension is high enough to detract from the flow of communication.

HOW LOGICAL AND RELATIONAL ISSUES INTERLOCK

How does an interviewer know when to deal with which kind of issue? People think and feel all the time: the brain and the body experiences always occur. Communication always has the logical and relational components. You have to work out for yourself two questions: (1) What am I like as a person—How do I function with my own thinking and feeling? (2) How does a particular interviewee appear to me to function with his own thinking and feeling? Success comes in a timely, sensitive matching of your own accessible thoughts and feelings and those of the other person. Some prefer to react to their own experiences logically first, and respond affectively only when logic does not work. Some believe that their experiences are logical—and only logical. Others, of course, react to their experiences affectively first, and relegate logic to a more limited function. Some treat their experiences as affective—and only affective. Rapport is a harmonious relationship in an interpersonal communication. It is based on each person's ability to answer the two questions above: he knows his own style, and he is sensitive to the other person's style. When two people have these abilities, they can work out the pattern of exchange of thoughts and feelings that works best for them.

In our culture, the trainee interviewer is likely not to be familiar with the range and depth of his emotional self. Hence the emphasis in this book on opening up your relational world. The challenge is not to get EE to change his mode of communicating to fit the style you prefer. The goal of effective interviewing is for you to learn to adapt to his preferred mode of communicating, to allow him to feel comfortable with it, and at the same time to gain his cooperation in sharing the information relevant to your purpose.

So much for the interpersonal theory. Now let us look specifically at the logical and relational issues that may arise during the practice interview.

LOGICAL AND RELATIONAL ISSUES IN PRACTICE INTERVIEWING

You may already have thought of some of the ways the logical and relational issues will affect you and your practice EE. Let's look first at some of the specific experiences of other trainee interviewers.

THE INTERVIEWER

The inexperienced ER encounters the relational issue of inclusion immediately, in two ways: (1) "Do I want to subject myself to all that is involved in this training in order to qualify as a competent depth interviewer?" and (2) "Do I feel like approaching friends or strangers to ask them to commit themselves to the anxiety-inducing process of a practice interview?" Before their first practice interview, trainees have expressed resistance to being included in many ways:

☐ "Do I have a right to ask someone about their private, personal feelings?"
☐ "My interviewee just won't show up for the appointments I have made. I can't get someone to help me."
☐ "Why don't you [teacher] lecture us on the good principles of interviewing, then we'll be able to apply them."
☐ "I didn't think I'd have to look at myself as a person in order to become a good interviewer. You want too much from me."

So much for the inclusion issue.

Especially threatening to the novice ER is the control issue. In your efforts to follow cues given by EE, you know that he may easily and subtly take over the direction and control of the interaction. You know you will be writing a critique of the interview—and that you will wince at signs that you have lost control. During the interview, the inexperienced ER's anxiety about control is manifested in the following ways:

Leading questions. ER asks questions that imply he already knows the answer.

Double-barreled questions. ER asks two or more questions before EE has a chance to answer the first one.

Interruptions. ER cuts off EE to redirect him or anticipate EE's answer.

Echo. ER repeats exactly what EE has just said—ER is momentarily lost and is fixated on a few of EE's words.

Assumptive statement. ER infers something not yet stated by EE.

Leading questions, interruptions, and assumptive statements can, of course, be used effectively by experienced ERs. When used by the novice, however, they usually indicate anxiety over controlling EE's responses.

Next, the relational issue of affection. The main challenge in practice interviewing is to get to the point where you can allow yourself to recognize and deal effectively with your affective reactions to EE. As you begin to feel "on top of" inclusion and control issues, you will have more "room" for this dimension. Although you may experience neither affection nor disaffection, likes and dislikes, yours and EE's are "happening" all the time. They may be indicated by little of what you or EE say, but the nonverbal information is there. You may be inadvertently ignoring many of your and EE's nonverbal cues because you are focusing on producing a "decent" interview. The burden of more cues than you can reasonably handle tends to make you tense and less competent at the logical level than you ordinarily can be. When the tension is most acute, you may find yourself

☐ Changing the subject to follow one cue before discussion of the prior topic is completed.
☐ Giving advice to EE about what he should do.
☐ Making assumptions privately and assumptive statements about what is causing a problem EE is describing.

Each of these responses reduces your tension. They move away from EE's feelings, by shifting to a more impersonal emphasis in the communication. These responses are typical of what we all do to reduce tension, and they come quickly, spontaneously. They interfere with your efforts to keep track of the discussion, recall your planned questions, and correctly formulate the next relevant question. As you become more comfortable with your own ways of reacting to the pressure of an interview, you will learn how to channel your tension into facilitative questions for EE, rather than move away from his feelings.

THE INTERVIEWEE
The volunteer EE, similarly, faces a gamut of logical and rela-

tional issues. When asked to volunteer, he may have mixed reactions to the issue of inclusion: (1) "I'd sure like to help if I can," but (2) "What am I getting myself in for? Can I trust this guy? What is he really trying to do? What will he do with the information I give him?"

Reading consciously or unconsciously to the issue of control, EE may attempt to diminish ER's power by

- ☐ Being vague; answering "I don't know."
- ☐ Asking ER a question about himself.
- ☐ Resorting to long, rambling monologues.
- ☐ Interrupting ER before he finishes a question.
- ☐ Asking ER to clarify his questions.
- ☐ Talking in a very low tone of voice so ER can just barely hear.

In addition, EE may send many nonverbal signals to ER to "ease off"—for example, frowning or wincing, sitting in a lackadaisical posture, or tapping a foot.

For interviewees also, issues of affection tend to be the most difficult issues. American EEs are likely to believe that they should reveal their inner feelings only to their closest friends. Even with close friends, inner feelings are apt to be guardedly and indirectly expressed. To reveal inner feelings to a stranger or a new acquaintance is thought to be immature. Some of the ways of avoiding a direct expression of feeling are

- ☐ Objectifying the feeling by expressing an opinion about the other person or object involved.
- ☐ Denying feelings.
- ☐ Avoiding use of the pronoun "I"; using "we" or "you" so that ER can't tell who belongs to the feeling or opinion.
- ☐ Crying or acting embarrassed.
- ☐ Asking to be excused for a minute.

If it is a novel experience for EE, he may be confused about what you really want to hear from him. And whether—and to what degree—you demonstrate that you are comfortable in this situation will largely determine how much of his feelings he will expose to you.

Now it is time to point out how the remainder of the book is organized to help you get into your practice interviewing.

USES OF THIS BOOK

We have said that you may be less aware of the relational than of the logical issues in interpersonal relations. The series of experiences and exercises offered in Chapter 2 may help you become more aware of how you react to the relational issues of inclusion, control, and affection. Once you have begun to see how you tend to react to these experiences, you are ready to consider the specific logical and relational aspects of interviewing. Figure 1 shows the types of critiques, the data used, the analyses and conclusions to be made in a complete evaluation of an interview.

Training exercises in the logical and relational issues are provided in Chapter 3. There is material on how to structure the beginning of an interview, how to deal with EE's efforts to overcontrol the interview, how to use your own personal reactions as a constructive guide for facilitating EE's responses, and how to recognize whether you are moving toward or away from EE's feelings. Chapter 3 will help you feel much more comfortable before you actually begin your first practice interview.

Your first step in practice interviewing will be to develop a plan of what information you will need, and what you will do with the information you hope to obtain. Chapter 4 explains both how to make such a plan and how the plan will help you evaluate the interview.

Hints about how to set up, conduct, and transcribe your practice interview are given in Chapter 5. There are several practical procedures that make interviewing a much easier task. Once the interview is conducted and transcribed, you are ready to do your critique of the manifest content and the interpersonal processes that occurred.

Chapter 6 shows you how to analyze the manifest content of

Figure 1. Diagram of the Interview Critique

Critique type	Data	Analysis	Conclusions
Manifest content (Chaps. 4, 6)	*Overt data* EE and ER verbalizations on transcript (Chap. 5)	Summary of data obtained and missing (Chaps. 4, 6)	Decisions about EE (output of interview) (Chap. 6) Evaluation of adequacy of ER's topical coverage (Chap. 6)
Interpersonal processes Logical process (information, opinion, and action issues) (Chaps. 1, 3)	*Overt and covert data* Transcript (Chap. 5) Audio or video tape (Chap. 3)	Input categories (Chap. 7) Critical interactions (Chap. 8)	EE's logical style and its impact on ER (Chap. 9) ER's logical style and its impact on outcome of interview (Chap. 9)
Relational process (inclusion, control, and affection issues) (Chaps. 1, 2, 3)	Transcript (Chap. 5) Audio or video tape (Chap. 3)	Input categories (Chap. 7) Critical interactions (Chap. 8)	EE's relational style and its impact on ER (Chap. 9) ER's relational style and its impact on outcome of interview (Chap. 9)
Balance between logical and relational processes (Chaps. 1, 3)	Transcript (Chap. 5) Audio or video tape (Chap. 3)	Input categories (Chap. 7) Critical interactions (Chap. 8)	EE's overall style and its impact on ER (Chap. 9) ER's overall style and its impact on outcome of interview (Chap. 9) ER's interviewing strengths and weaknesses (Chap. 9)
Impact of setting (Chaps. 3, 4, 5)	ER observes (Chap. 3) Roles in plan (Chap. 4)	Description of EE behavior (Chap. 9) Description of interview setting (Chap. 9)	Impact of setting on EE (Chap. 9) Impact of setting on ER (Chap. 9)

your interview. As noted earlier, analysis of the manifest content permits you to compare information you actually got with the information you intended to obtain. You will be able to answer such questions as (1) For each planned topic, how much information did you actually get? (2) How thoroughly did you cover each planned topic? (3) What conclusions can you accurately make from the information you obtained? Once the manifest content analysis is completed, you will be ready to move on to the process analysis, which is explained in Chapters 7 and 8.

Chapter 7 treats the first step in the process analysis: the categorization of the kinds of questions you asked and the kinds of responses EE gave you. This categorization will enable you to undertake other analyses of the logical and relational interactions that occurred.

Chapter 8 explains how to evaluate your reactions to the logical and relational issues as they came up and your—and EE's—logical and relational style. For example, you will learn to identify the signals of discontinuous communication, and what you did or did not do about them.

How to combine the manifest content analysis and the interaction process analyses so you can summarize your strengths and weaknesses as an interviewer is described in Chapter 9. This summary will serve as a guide in later practice interviews. Comparison of your skill levels in the first and second interviews will indicate how much you have progressed.

The Appendix provides the transcript and critique of an interview conducted by one of my students. You will find it helpful to study this material before you read the next chapter. In the text, examples of how to do each step are taken from the Appendix and from other interviews done by my students.

2

EXPERIENCING RELATIONAL ISSUES

It usually is difficult for trainee ERs to identify relational issues they may be experiencing. These issues are more covert than overt. In our culture, the norm is not to express feelings directly in most relationships. If you are not aware of the feelings, you cannot identify the relational issues. This chapter offers exercises designed to help you become more aware of the feelings involved in relational issues.

EXPERIENCING INCLUSION

Inclusion, the first relational issue, refers to how much you feel *in* or *out* of a relationship. Reflect on a recent experience in which you entered a room of strangers. What did you do? How did you feel? Stop and try to recall how you felt. Close your eyes for a minute or two. How did you feel just before you entered the room—before any of the strangers saw you? Almost everyone experiences tension or anxiety at the beginning of such an experience. Some convert the anxiety into assertive behavior: they move into the room, introduce themselves, and rapidly become at ease. Others are, or seem to be, more diffident. They wait for someone else to introduce them. They tend to stay (physically) on the fringe of the group. It is more difficult for them to reduce their anxiety and feel included. Findings from proxemics, the study of how people use and are affected by time and space, are useful in understanding inclusion phenomena. (See the reference for proxemics and other types of nonverbal research in the Annotated Bibliography for Chapter 3.)

VIEW IT FROM A WINDOW

Next time you have the opportunity, enter a group of strangers and note how you are reacting. After a few minutes, find an excuse to leave the room. Observe the group from outside the room—through a window, if possible. Note how you feel when outside. Compare your reactions when outside and inside the group.

Example. In a class discussion on interpersonal relations, one student was noted to prefer to sit well outside (2 or 3 feet) the perimeter of the circle of the other chairs. The teacher asked the student how much he felt "in" the group. The student replied: "I don't really know." The teacher asked the student if he would like to experience more directly how much he felt included in the group. The student agreed. The group formed a close circle, standing. The student first stood inside the circle, then slowly walked to a far corner of the room. He said he didn't find much difference. The teacher asked him to try it again. When inside the circle, the student said he did feel some tension in his abdomen. After going to the far corner again, the student reflected: "I am more comfortable here. I guess I really prefer to be outside of this group."

Explanation. Going through the physical movement of being "in" and "out" of the group helped the student become more aware of his inner reactions to the experience. When later he discussed his reactions, he stated that he did tend to keep people at a distance, preferring not to risk personal exposure—especially with classroom peers with whom he felt he was competing. Hence he was committed to limited involvement in the group—just enough to accomplish the cognitive objectives of the course, but not enough to engage in personal encounter with other class members. He reported that he felt more comfortable with his low need for inclusion after going through the exercise. In some instances, we tend to repress the feelings associated with the issue of inclusion. Feelings are repressed because of an apparent conflict with a teacher's expectations. The feelings may be elicited by deliberately going through the physical movements that represent the contrast of being "in" or "out" of a group.

EXPERIENCING CONTROL

The second relational issue is control. Control refers to how much influence you perceive that you wield at a given moment in a relationship. The underlying feelings are connected with the position you sense you hold: from "on top" to "equal" to "on bottom." Feelings of exhilaration, anger, and disappointment experienced in competitive sports are examples of emotional reactions to the issue of control. Here is an exercise which will show you the control process.

THE RUBBER BAND EXERCISE

Stand face-to-face with a partner; raise both hands so that your left palm mirrors his right palm and your right palm mirrors his left palm. Fingers are extended, but relaxed. Your hands are about two to three inches from his. (Do not touch hands during the exercise.) Now say to your partner: "Pretend there are rubber bands around each pair of hands—your right and my left, and your left and my right. We are to move our hands in any way we wish, remembering we are to pretend there are rubber bands around each pair. Do not talk for the next three minutes." You and your partner move in any fashion you each choose. After two or three minutes, stop by mutual agreement (or have someone time you). Discuss with your partner how each reacted to the other's movements. Some questions to pose are: Who led? How did he lead? How fast did he lead? How high, low, broad were his movements? Did the leadership change? How did it change? How did you react to being the follower? How did you follow? What did you watch while you were following (for example, did you focus on his eyes using peripheral vision, or did you look directly at his hands)?

Example. A sensitivity group trainer did the rubber band exercise with Judy. The trainer started as the leader, moving his hands slowly in ever-increasing circles, symmetrically. Judy followed well. The trainer paused in the starting position, nonverbally indicating to Judy to lead. Judy did not elect to lead. The trainer noticed that Judy watched only his right hand. The trainer led again, using asymmetrical movements. Judy frowned and looked into the trainer's eyes pleadingly. The trainer continued to lead, resuming the symmetrical movements. Discussing his reactions, the trainer said he was frustrated by the way in which Judy obtained the information about how she was to follow—she limited him by looking only at his right hand. Judy reflected a moment, then said: "That's right. I don't like to lead. But I only like to follow in certain ways. Say! That's exactly what my husband tells me! I want him to lead, but I'll only follow in the ways I prefer, and it makes it hard for him to accomplish what he wants!"

Explanation. In this exercise instructions are vague and verbal interactions are not permitted as a means of reducing ambiguity. Under these conditions the partners experience more vividly the feelings involved in the control process. This simple exercise elicits from some their usual response to control issues: a preference for leading, following, or seeking equality (in this case, a free interchange of leadership and followership). It may point out to a few people their awkwardness in performing motor tasks that are to be coordinated with another person's movements. Typically, the person who first follows begins to feel frustration after 20 to 30 seconds, and actively seeks to take over control if his partner does not of his own accord shift roles. The person who first leads tends to be less aware of his reactions to the initial resolution of the control issue: he typically feels at ease and is pleased with the experience. Participants usually are not aware of the methods by which they obtain information about the partner's movements. Those who focus on the partner's eyes and use peripheral vision—both right and left—tend to be more at ease with the exercise. Those who look at one or both of the partner's hands tend to find the exercise more difficult and may discount the experience by saying: "I couldn't figure out what motion to do with the rubber band."

EXPERIENCING AFFECTION

Affection, the third relational issue, refers to what you feel—love, hate, approval, disapproval—about the other person. It is most vividly portrayed by how the feeling might be converted into action: do you want to hug him, hit him, withdraw from him, or ignore him? Affectionate or antagonistic feelings may have a major impact on how you react to what another person is saying or doing. Many barriers to good communication arise from the underlying feelings each person has about the other. Because the strongest of feelings tend to be involved in affectional issues caution should be used in deciding which exercises are appropriate. Following is an exercise of moderate intensity.

VERBALIZING POSITIVE FEELINGS

From a group of friends who understand the purpose of the exercise, ask for one volunteer who will be given positive feedback about his impact on others. The others speak to the question "What do I like about you?" Comments may range from observations of physical characteristics to ways of behaving to values reflected in the person's behavior.

Example. Jim agreed to have fellow members of a graduate psychology course in interviewing give him positive feedback about his impact on others. Comments included: "I like the positive way you react when we're doing something together. You have lots of energy." "Yes, I noticed that, too. You really 'sparkle' with enthusiasm once you've started to act." "I like your curly hair—it looks so yummy to touch." "You're smart. You do well in class." "You are unassuming." Jim found the build-up of positive feedback quite strong. He began to tear. He was deeply touched by the positive acceptance others expressed.

Explanation. Usually others express to their friends their negative disaffection more readily than their positive approval. To experience nothing but positive affection for several minutes is very moving, when the person perceives others' comments as genuine. We usually get mostly nonverbal cues from others about their feelings for us. Rarely are the feelings spoken. Nonverbal cues often have some degree of ambiguity, especially when two persons are interacting over a mutual task—as in interviewing. A smile may mean: "I like you." A slightly different smile may mean: "Take it easy. You are pressuring me too much."

EXPERIENCING INTERPERSONAL SPACE

Each of us, from moment to moment, has a definite but usually covert sense of the interpersonal "space" around us. Sometimes we want others to be in our space. Sometimes we don't. Sometimes we have feelings of expansiveness and allow almost anyone to intrude in our space. Sometimes we have feelings of disdain and reject bids from almost anyone to enter into our space. A fundamental skill for ER is being aware of his and EE's space during the interview. The following simple exercise helps vivify the phenomenon of our interpersonal space.

MILLING AND EXPLORING SPACE

Ask people who agree to share the experience to meet in a room. Begin by clearing the room of objects that might be tripped over. Instruct participants to keep their eyes shut and not to talk throughout the exercise. Participants then stand in the open space, close their eyes, and wander about the room at random. This is called "milling." By prearranged signal, after one to three minutes of milling, participants seat themselves on the floor, keeping their eyes shut. For another two or three minutes, they explore their space with their hands. After exploring their space, participants open their eyes and remain where they seated themselves. They then discuss their reactions to the milling, the exploration of their space, and especially their reactions to touching and being touched by others.

Examples of typical reactions. In the milling, some enjoy the experience of touching, and some are neutral or abhor it. The decision and initial reactions involve the inclusion issue. Later, issues of both control and affection are involved. After participants are seated, the interaction process slows down and they may discover how they react when others intrude into their space by touching them. Reactions range from "I liked it when you held my hand" to "I moved away because I didn't want you going after me!" Discuss the size of the space each person perceived. Some explore only the floor immediately in front of them —or wherever they find freedom to move without touching another person. Others are more expansive and move their hands up and down, behind them, both right and left. Reaction to touching others is significant: some recoil immediately; others continue to explore by moving up the other person's arm or leg or by feeling his head. Reaction to being touched by others is also significant: some freeze; some jerk or slowly move away; some reciprocate. Location in the room may tell something of feelings of inclusion. Those who feel outside the group will tend to locate on the fringe (in one instance, members of a faculty group fled the room!); those who feel most "in" tend to locate in what they imagine to be the center of the cleared space.

Explanation. This exercise may invoke reactions to all three relational issues. It is the sensation of one's own space and another's space that defines the range of possible solutions to the relational issues. If ER feels free to move only in space unoccupied by other persons, he will tend to avoid personal topics in an interview—and be unsuccessful in eliciting EE's feelings. If ER feels "in" the relationship with EE, he will be freer to facilitate EE's expression of feelings.

The exercise provides clearcut examples both of the need to control other's invasion of your space and the enjoyment or rejection of mutual expression of affection by touching. Research in proxemics supports these observations.

DIARY OF FEELINGS

Keep a brief record of your strongest feelings and moods over a period of two to four days. Try to record each feeling as soon after it occurs as possible. And make a note of your observable behavior related to the feeling. Here are some examples.

Feeling	Observable behavior
1. Relaxed	Sitting at ease, arms and legs calm
2. Alive	Walk briskly, alert to environment, smiling
3. Tired (feel heart pounding)	Walk slowly, head bent over, shoulders drooping, eyes half shut
4. Weary (eyes aching, mind wandering)	Look up from book, look around room
5. Nervous (face hot, hands cold, wet)	Short, uncoordinated arm and leg movements
6. Exhausted (eyes weathered)	Face sullen, gait haphazardous
7. Angry	Snapped at wife, biting teeth, clenching jaw
8. Enthused	Head up, quick body movements, eyes wide open
9. Welcome surprise (lifting of the stomach, sudden surge of energy)	Smiling, talk more
10. Irritation (heated neck, knot in stomach, urge to hit)	Face reddened, words clipped, laugh disgustedly, then silent with shake of head

Note that in some instances the physical sensation is depicted as well as the feeling tone of the experience. You will find that some feelings result in easily observable behavior, others do not. If you discover that you are not aware of the observable behavior prompted by different feelings, try looking in a mirror. Get acquainted with how mood affects facial expression: try out your happy look, your sad look, your angry look, your confused look, and so forth.

In the interview, you are a participant-observer. To help develop more objective observational skills, the next exercise casts you in the role of nonparticipant observer.

WATCH A STRANGER

In a public place where you can watch a stranger for a few minutes, note three things: (1) the stranger's nonverbal behavior, (2) the inferences you make about his internal feeling state, and (3) your feelings about the role of nonparticipant observer. Here is an example.

Role: Teacher
Place: Classroom

Nonverbal behavior	*Observer's inferences*
1. Scratched forehead	Perplexed on what and how to present material
2. Hand on hip, leaning back	Showing his authority over students
3. Half smile	Nervous
4. Hand in pocket, scratches face, scratches side	Lack of poise and self-confidence

Observer's feelings

I had empathy for his attempts to communicate with us, his students. I also had respect for his intelligence and knowledge. I was distracted by his nervous movements. I was turned off by his groping for more poise and confidence. It was easy to be an observer, as a member of a class of 25 students.

Most report that it is easier to keep a diary of one's own feelings than to be a nonparticipant observer. In interviewing, we seek a balance between self-awareness and sensitivity to the other person. Practice more if either type of sensitivity is difficult for you.*

Now we turn to how the relational processes—and the parallel logical processes—affect you in the interviewing process. Chapter 3 describes role-plays that will help you get into the actual dynamics of interviewing.

---

* The Annotated Bibliography for this chapter lists a number of texts designed to help the individual gain in self-awareness and sensitivity.

3

TAKING THE PLUNGE: ROLE-PLAYS IN DEPTH INTERVIEWING

Chapters 1 and 2 have equipped you with a theoretical and experiential picture of the logical and relational processes in interpersonal relations. It is time to take the plunge. How do you react to the relational issues in an actual interview? How can you tell if the logical process is ineffective? What EE behavior throws you off? What can you do about EE behavior that undermines the interview?

What do you need to get started? First, a quiet setting, with comfortable seating, and an audio or video recorder. Second, someone to interact with you in the role-plays. Ask a fellow employee, a fellow student, or a friend to help you. If your helper also is a trainee-interviewer, you may alternate ER and EE roles. An observer is a good idea, too. In a classroom, several students may be observers.

Good role-playing occurs when you know what you are looking for, and when you, EE, and observer are enthused about the practice and relaxed about critiquing each other. Another hint: Keep it short. Two to four minutes of role-playing is often enough to illustrate a particular point.

Following is a "key" to the criteria for successful role-playing. If you or your partners are unsure about any of these steps, practice them.

1. Make sure your recording equipment is recording—*now*.
2. Pick a partner. Discuss how each of you feels about doing role-playing.
3. Pick a role-playing problem you both agree is relevant.
4. Agree on which criteria you will evaluate at the end of the role-play.
5. Give each role-player a few minutes to get oriented to his role.
6. Do the role-play. Keep to two to four minutes. If there is an observer, have him time and stop the role-play.
7. At the end of the role-play, give ER and EE a couple of minutes to share their reactions to the experience.
8. Listen to the playback. ER and EE may use the observation sheet (Figure 2) to take notes.
9. Discuss data first. Then discuss inferences and overall impressions.

CRITERIA FOR EVALUATING LOGICAL AND RELATIONAL PROCESSES

Chapter 1 described the earmarks for effective logical and relational communications. (See pp. 4 and 10.) What can we look for in an actual interview? First translate those earmarks into simpler terms of observable behaviors. Figure 2 is a worksheet for observing an interview. Adapt this sample worksheet to suit your specific type of interview or make copies of it for you and your helpers. Here are some specific ways to use the observer's sheet.

LOGICAL CONTINUITY

The two key verbal behaviors to watch for are a sudden change in topic (item 1 in the data sheet of Figure 2) and a sudden change in logical level (item 2). Take notes on ER and EE behaviors as follows. For item 1: enter previous logical level (for example, opinion) and new logical level (for example, information). After the role-play, the observer may jot down other observations about ER's and EE's logical skills—behaviors that

Figure 2. Data Sheet for Observing Logical and Relational Processes

Date	Observer's name		
		Interviewer's name	*Interviewee's name*
Logical Continuity			
1. Abrupt change in topic			
2. Abrupt change in logical level			
3. Comments on logical skill			
Relational Expressions			
4. Verbal, direct			
5. Verbal, indirect			
6. Comments on verbal skill			
7. Nonverbal, direct			
8. Nonverbal, indirect			
9. Comments on nonverbal skill			

helped and hindered the logical process. A key ER behavior is the types of questions asked—open-ended or closed. A key EE behavior is how organized his answers are.

RELATIONAL EXPRESSIONS

Jot down examples of verbal expressions you believe are either direct (item 4) or indirect (item 5)—expressions you interpret to be either direct statements of the speaker's feelings or statements that have emotional overtones but do not clearly reveal how the speaker feels. (See Davitz, 1969* for a dictionary of

---

* Literature on analysis of emotional content is annotated on p. 185.

feelings.) In item 6, note other verbal behaviors that helped or hindered ER's and EE's expression of feelings. Keep items 4, 5, and 6 to the content of the speech (nonverbal characteristics of speech are rated below).

NONVERBAL RELATIONAL EXPRESSIONS

Enter nonverbal expressions you think are either direct (item 7) or indirect (item 8). Here are common nonverbal behaviors to watch for, and examples of how they may be direct or indirect.

Tone of voice—loud or soft?

Direct	Loud when angry or excited; soft when sad or affectionate
Indirect	Loud when he says he's relaxed; soft when he says he's angry

Tone of voice—warm or cold (or, relaxed or tense)?

Direct	Warm when he expresses closeness; cold when he expresses distance
Indirect	Warm when he expresses conflict; cold when he expresses warm feeling

Eye contact—where is he looking?

Direct	Looks at other person when he tries to cooperate
Indirect	Looks at other person when he says he is not interested; looks at ceiling when he says he is

Body position—which way is his trunk leaning?

Direct	Leans forward when he says he's involved; leans back when he refuses to cooperate
Indirect	Sits upright, stiffly, when he claims he's relaxed; sits back, nonchalantly, when he says he's involved

Gestures (arms and hands)

Direct	Arm movement follows verbal expression
Indirect	Nervous or unrelated arm or hand movements; note especially if arms crossed, hands clasped

Facial expressions

Direct	Smiles when he says he's happy; frowns when he says he's mad
Indirect	Smiles when he says he's mad; looks tense when he says he's relaxed

Interruptions

Direct	Explains reason for interruption
Indirect	Interrupts without appearing to know he's interrupting

Pauses

Direct	After ER asks question, waits for EE to answer, gives EE at least two to three seconds to answer; after EE gives answer, EE waits for two to three seconds to get feedback from ER
Indirect	No pauses—rushed pace; or awkward pause by ER while he tries to word the next question

In item 9, put down notes on other aspects of nonverbal behaviors that seemed to have a facilitative or hindering effect on the interview. Here, you might comment on the range of nonverbal behavior: from very limited (like a corpse) to medium variety to wide range (like an actor). You might also note the intensity level: from little impact to high impact on the other person. A rich array of findings is now available on nonverbal cues. (See the Annotated Bibliography.)

You will find that with a little practice, this observation process generates a wealth of data. Soon you will be ready to make some broader judgments about the logical and relational processes in the interview. The following questions will help you assess the overall interview:

1. Compare ER's nonverbal expressions with his verbal expressions. Which were more dominant? How congruent was his nonverbal behavior with his verbal behavior?

2. Compare EE's nonverbal expressions with his verbal expressions. Which were more dominant? How congruent was his nonverbal behavior with his verbal behavior?

3. How aware did ER appear to be of EE's thinking and feeling? How did ER show his awareness, or lack of it?

4. How aware did EE appear to be of ER's thinking and feeling? How did EE show his awareness, or lack of it?

5. Describe ER's overall style of thinking and feeling. Which mode of expression was most evident? How well did ER shift from logical to emotional expression? How did ER appear to react to the relational issues—inclusion, control, affection?

6. Describe EE's overall style of thinking and feeling. Which mode of expression was most evident? How well did EE shift from logical to emotional expression? How did EE appear to react to the relational issues—inclusion, control, affection?

7. What degree of rapport, logically and relationally, was achieved?

8. How much of the intended purpose of the interview was achieved?

So much for the criteria you may use, and for ways to collect the data. Next we consider what role-plays may be useful for getting into the dynamics of the interview.

ROLE-PLAY: STRONG PERSONAL FEELINGS

Sometimes EE has very strong personal feelings or opinions about a topic. ER tries to give EE enough opportunity to express them. It is a challenge to ER to keep his own personal feelings or opinions from overt involvement in the interaction.

Pick a topic that immediately conjurs up a strong reaction in both ER and EE. These have worked in classes with undergraduates:

1. If you now had the opportunity to take LSD, would you do it?

2. Describe what happened to you the last time someone became angry at you.
3. How did you react the last time a person of the opposite sex tried to be close to you?
4. Describe the happiest experience you have had in the last year.
5. Describe what you did the last time you became angry at someone.
6. What has been your most difficult job? Why?
7. If your neighbors asked you to join forces with them to prevent further integration of an "undesirable race" in your neighborhood, what would you do?

After trying the role-playing, you will probably find the relational data of most interest. This exercise is intended to help both ER and EE get feedback on how directly they express their feelings.

ROLE-PLAY: POLITICAL OPINIONS

Every adult has a series of fairly well-reasoned opinions on a variety of topics—often political or social issues. In this role-play, the interviewer is challenged to get a complete logical picture of the information base, the specific kinds of assumptions, opinions, and projections into the future, and the specific actions EE may intend to take on a given topic. Hence this exercise emphasizes the logical processes. Here are some suggested topics.

1. The Vietnam war. How much does EE know about the background and current extent of U.S. involvement in Vietnam? What are EE's specific opinions about the reasoning for our being there? What actions does EE think the U.S. should take in the near future? Why? What personal action does EE think he will take in the near future? Why?
2. Conflicts in the schools. How much does EE know about the development of social conflicts in schools? What are EE's specific opinions about the radical student organiza-

tions and the variety of college administrators' policies in regard to demonstrations and violence on the campus? What actions does EE think students, college administrators, and community law enforcement agencies should take in the near future? Why? What personal action does EE think he would take were he invited to join in a protest? Why?

This role-play takes ten to twenty minutes. Agree on a time limit in advance.

ROLE-PLAY: OFF TO A GOOD START

Is there a "best" approach to starting an interview? Yes! If you attend first to three things, the interview almost always will go better: (a) review the purpose, (b) scan the overall topic, and (c) ask a broad informational question first. In reviewing the purpose, ER reminds EE why the interview is being conducted and explains again the ethical provisions for the use of the tape and transcript, if any are to be made. To scan the overall topic, ER repeats the general subject matter he hopes to get EE to comment about. The initial broad informational question is called a DESCRIPTIVE question. In effect EE is asked to relate an experience, in his own style, to ER. With practice, you will find the specific wording for each of the three ingredients that best fits your style of communicating.

This role-play enables you to experience the contrast between a well-started and a poorly-started interview. You and EE pick a topic of interest to EE—a vivid experience which presumably has had a definite impact on his life. It might be a tragedy—a bad accident, the death of a parent or spouse, or a failure in school. Or it might be a positive experience—winning a scholarship, succeeding in sports competition, or enjoying a period of personal growth.

The procedure is to do two starts. For the first, ER begins with closed-ended FACT ("How old were you when it happened?") or OPINION ("Do you think the experience helped you?") questions. After two or three minutes in this vein, stop the interview. Begin again with a review of PURPOSE and ETHICS

—for example, "As we discussed, this interview is for my benefit, to get practice and feedback in my techniques. The information will be kept confidential, and no one except me will know your name. Only I will listen to the tape, unless I have your prior approval for someone else to listen to it."

Next, scan the overall TOPIC—for example, "Today, I'd like to talk with you about your reactions to your four years of work experience in the juvenile home: what your easy and difficult tasks are, what progress you have made in introducing your new ideas, and what future plans you have." Finally, begin the questioning with a broad DESCRIPTIVE question—for example, "First, I'd like to know what led you to consider the position you now have. How did you happen to apply for this position?" Stop the role-play after EE has given his first few answers.

Now compare ER and EE reactions to the two different beginnings. Differences may show up in both the logical and the relational processes. Novice ERs may find it beneficial to do at least four or five such practice beginnings. We assume you now are convinced about the best way to begin! The approach assumes relatively equal EE and ER communication skills. If skills are markedly unequal, EE may do better with more limited questions until he begins to feel at ease.

ROLE-PLAY: THE SUPERTALKER

Some people control an interaction by talking too fast and too long on whatever topics appeal to them. This is a common fear among new ERs: what can they do if they get a supertalker?

Pick an EE who feels he can take the part of a supertalker. How should the supertalker behave? He starts with ER's first question and gives a relevant answer. But before ER can pose another question, EE is off on a related topic, and keeps talking just fast enough and loud enough to make it awkward for ER to interrupt. EE is strongly controlling the interview. He does this supertalking for about three to five minutes.

This role-play may illustrate both logical and relational processes. At the logical level, it may show how EE subtly changes the topic, and how EE shifts the logical level just frequently enough to keep ER in the dark about what he might try next. At the relational level, if EE controls strongly enough, both EE and ER may begin to show definite verbal and nonverbal expressions of the tension. We have found that trainees tend to be pretty hard on each other, so cut the role-playing as soon as an obvious level of tension is reached.

After seeing how it goes the first time, help ER determine alternative behaviors he might try to tone down the supertalker. Then give ER a chance to practice some of these alternatives.

ROLE-PLAY: THE UNDERDOG

Some people control an interaction by not talking enough. They give short, seemingly factual, unemotional answers. Nonverbally, they convey either confusion or actual unwillingness to cooperate. This also is a common fear among new interviewers: what can they do if EE is unwilling or unable to express himself?

Instructions to EE: give only one-to-four-word answers. Use "I don't know" if an answer would have to be longer. Try to keep emotionally neutral.

This role-play may illustrate mostly the relational issues of inclusion and control. Inclusion problems are shown by EE in his inability or unwillingness to participate. Control problems are introduced by EE's underplaying and thus frustrating ER's attempts to get adequate interaction going.

After seeing how it goes the first time, help ER determine alternative means he might use to get the underdog to talk more. Then give ER a chance to practice some of these alternatives.

ROLE-PLAY: GOOD PROBING

A successful ER can both follow a plan and show good follow-up with any cues given by EE. It takes practice to do both. Typically, inexperienced ERs are too preoccupied with their plan and miss cues given by EE. A series of role-plays will help you both follow up cues (probe) and follow your plan.

First, do an interview on a general topic (as in the off-to-a-good-start role-play above) without having a planned outline.

Start with a broad DESCRIPTIVE question, then base all further questions on EE's initial DESCRIPTIVE response. See how long you can go without introducing a new topic. Stop, and critique your efficiency in probing. What cues did you pick up on? What cues did you miss?

Second, arrange an interview on a topic (as in the off-to-a-good-start role-play above). Make up an outline of three or four specific items you think are logically related to the person's experience. For example, if the topic is the effects of a failure in college, subtopics might include the following items:

1. Describe the situation in which the failure occurred.
2. What does EE think were the causes in him and in the situation?
3. What did EE do after experiencing the failure? How did he feel?
4. What impact does EE think the failure now is having on him?

Now do the second interview, trying to keep a balance between good probing and accomplishing your preplanned outline.

The critique of the second interview may focus on the logical processes and the relational process of control. Notice your efficiency in probing and in achieving the intended topical coverage. Analyze what logical and emotional conditions in you helped and hindered your efficiency.

ROLE-PLAY: EE SUDDENLY EMOTES
Beginning ERs are thrown off guard when EE spontaneously expresses a personal reaction. ERs usually have the set that personal reactions will be hard to get! In many cases, EEs are surprisingly willing to expose themselves. ERs often find themselves reluctant to probe in personal areas. So what does ER do? He tends to change the topic or shift the logical level from personal exposure to more impersonal, factual questions. The effect is to get away from embarrassment and the potential involvement in EE's affective state.

This role-play may be set up as was the strong-personal-feelings role-play. Ask EE to identify a topic about which he has had vivid emotional reactions he is willing to expose. First, ER may want to see how he typically reacts to EE's strong expression of feeling. Second, ER may want to try different responses which might better facilitate the interchange.

This role-play focuses on the relational processes. Look especially for ER's verbal and nonverbal reactions when EE expresses a strong feeling.

SCRIPT PRACTICE: HOW TO WORD QUESTIONS

How well do you find yourself wording the next question? Below is a practice script, with blank space for you to jot down the next question you believe should be asked. Explain to your partner why you think that question would be good, both logically and relationally. Then critique the actual ER's question in terms of EE's response. If you prefer, your partner can read EE's responses out loud, and you can verbalize your next question. Here's the script (taken from a practice interview).

ER: *(After explaining purpose)* I thought maybe I'd like to talk with you a little bit about your present marriage.

EE: Uh huh.

ER: And how you feel your experience with Michael and with Jim may affect your marriage now.

EE: Oh, boy! *(Laughs)* Have you got a long tape?

ER: [Your next question _____. The actual question ER asked is the following] *(Laughs)* Oh, this is something you've given some thought to?

EE: Boy, have I given some thought to it! You mean, how it has affected this marriage?

ER: [Your next question: _____. Actual response ER gave] Yes.

EE: Well, first of all, it's grown me up. I feel a lot more wiser. Ah, I'd say that . . . uh . . . everyone needs a basis to go on, sort of, and my first marriage . . . well, to start with Michael now . . . *(Pauses, hesitant)*

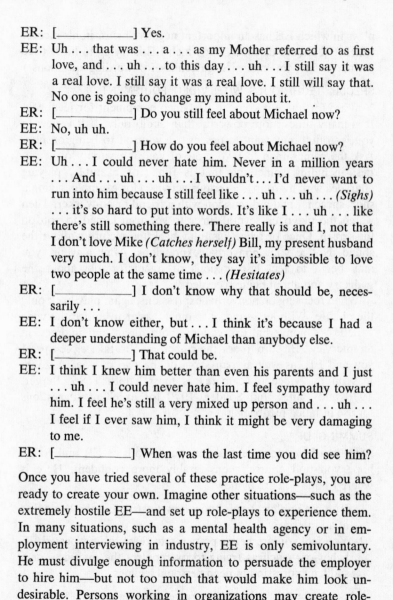

ER: [_____] Yes.

EE: Uh . . . that was . . . a . . . as my Mother referred to as first love, and . . . uh . . . to this day . . . uh . . . I still say it was a real love. I still say it was a real love. I still will say that. No one is going to change my mind about it.

ER: [_____] Do you still feel about Michael now?

EE: No, uh uh.

ER: [_____] How do you feel about Michael now?

EE: Uh . . . I could never hate him. Never in a million years . . . And . . . uh . . . uh . . . I wouldn't . . . I'd never want to run into him because I still feel like . . . uh . . . uh . . . *(Sighs)* . . . it's so hard to put into words. It's like I . . . uh . . . like there's still something there. There really is and I, not that I don't love Mike *(Catches herself)* Bill, my present husband very much. I don't know, they say it's impossible to love two people at the same time . . . *(Hesitates)*

ER: [_____] I don't know why that should be, necessarily . . .

EE: I don't know either, but . . . I think it's because I had a deeper understanding of Michael than anybody else.

ER: [_____] That could be.

EE: I think I knew him better than even his parents and I just . . . uh . . . I could never hate him. I feel sympathy toward him. I feel he's still a very mixed up person and . . . uh . . . I feel if I ever saw him, I think it might be very damaging to me.

ER: [_____] When was the last time you did see him?

Once you have tried several of these practice role-plays, you are ready to create your own. Imagine other situations—such as the extremely hostile EE—and set up role-plays to experience them. In many situations, such as a mental health agency or in employment interviewing in industry, EE is only semivoluntary. He must divulge enough information to persuade the employer to hire him—but not too much that would make him look undesirable. Persons working in organizations may create role-plays in which EE has an important negative factor in his record, which ER should discover, but which EE is trying to hide. (See Payne, 1951* for extensive guidelines for wording questions.)

SPECIAL TECHNIQUES WITH VIDEO EQUIPMENT

You are fortunate if you can use video equipment for feedback. It is many times more powerful than audio only. If it is new to you, you first may want to desensitize yourself to being on film. Ask the cameraman to take shots of you in a variety of activities, including something that is fun (for example, playing charades with a group), a serious activity (for example, giving a short speech), and a discussion with a friend or co-worker. Then watch the playback several times to get accustomed to you on the screen. Once or twice, just play back the picture without the sound. Notice your nonverbal expressions. After a while, you may begin to feel less anxious or uncomfortable about the gadgetry and about being recorded.

When focusing on nonverbal expressions, again play back only the picture. Without sound, it is much easier to notice the wide varieties of nonverbal expressions, both direct and indirect, in an interview. Be sure to ask the cameraman to take close-ups of you and EE, as well as pan shots of the two of you. A zoom lens on the videocon (camera) is most helpful. (See Berger, 1970 and Bailey and Souder, 1970 for excellent suggestions for use of taped feedback.)

SUMMING UP

After you have done several role-plays, both as ER and EE, I hope you find yourself considerably more confident. Here is where I hope you are by now.

1. You are confident you know how to structure the beginning of an interview.
2. You feel you are better prepared to react to unexpected EE behavior—such as trying to overcontrol the interview or a sudden expression of deep personal feelings.

---

* See Annotated Bibliography on survey interviewing pp. 183–184.

3. You have a concrete idea of how logical and relational issues show up in your and EE's behavior.
4. You have found that your own personal feelings, whether or not expressed to EE, help you decide what to do next as ER.
5. You can recognize when you are covertly moving toward or away from EE's expressions of his ideas and his feelings.
6. You recognize the impact of different types of questions—broad or open-ended versus narrow or closed—and are beginning to be flexible in using both types.
7. You know how to start an interview: how to word the purpose, scan the topic, and begin with a descriptive question.
8. You are aware of when you are following EE's cues well, and when you are staying too close to your predetermined outline.
9. You are more aware of how to get EE to clarify his ideas by including informational, opinion, and action-oriented questions.
10. You have a rough reading on your overall interviewing style and on which logical and relational processes you need more practice. You may want to stop now, and list the skills you find you already have. Then list the skills you want to practice some more.

As you progress through the rest of the book, you may find more situations to try out in role-playing. Sometimes one problem area may be especially difficult for you. A little more practice will help.

4

HOW TO PLAN A DEPTH INTERVIEW

Now that you have developed some confidence in your sensitivities and your abilities in conducting a depth interview, it is time to learn how to make a plan. The plan focuses on the manifest content of the interview: the information needed from EE (EE inputs) and the inferences to be made about the information obtained (outputs). The planned EE inputs help you formulate the topics you need to cover and the specific questions you may need to ask. The planned outputs indicate the nature of the professional judgments you will expect to be able to make from EE inputs you hope to obtain.

Without a prior commitment to an intended result, it is a cat-and-mouse game to try to evaluate your ER behavior. Hence, the procedure will be for you to develop your intended results in the plan, then evaluate the manifest and latent content in terms of what you hoped to accomplish.

What should be included in your write-up of a plan for a practice depth interview? These are important:

A. The role relationships of ER and EE
1. ER's role
2. EE's role

B. Formulation of the problem
   1. Description of the problem
   2. Information available prior to the interview
C. Outputs: analyses, conclusions, or decisions to be made from the data collected from EE. The training procedure in this book stops with the first intellectual step in formulating output conclusions—the preparation of an accurate summary of data obtained. If you are interested in later intellectual steps involved in making inferences or abstractions, see Levy (1963)* and Sundberg and Tyler (1962).
D. EE inputs: Data needed from EE to accomplish the intended outputs.

An example of a plan follows. This interview—called the "Jim Smith Interview"—is used to illustrate each step of the procedure. (The complete Jim Smith interview plan, transcript, and analysis is in the Appendix.) Examples from other practice interviews are cited to illustrate special cases. In the material below, explanations of each part of the plan appear in boldface type. The written plan, of course, is similar to one you will write.

A. THE ROLE RELATIONSHIPS OF ER AND EE

1. *ER's role.* ER is a senior college student in a course on interviewing. ER is an acquaintance of EE. They have not seen each other for several years. ER needs an interview to practice for his interviewing course. ER is expecting EE to cooperate in the interview in order to give ER interview experience. ER thinks EE is facing a situation which EE needs to resolve.

> **Describe the specific actual roles. Do not use fictitious roles. Students in training should not call themselves clinicians. Employees who are performing actual interviewing duties should so identify themselves. Give facts of ER's situation: student, employee, etc. Also state past relationships, if any, of ER and EE. If no past relationship, state how ER made contact with EE. State**

* See p. 184.

what ER expects of EE, and why ER thinks the interview may be of benefit to EE.

2. *EE's role.* EE is a 20-year-old male, high-school dropout, now working as a day laborer. ER has contacted EE by phone, and explained briefly the purpose of the interview. EE stated he is willing to start the interview, but is unsure how fully he will want to cooperate. No specifices of the interview plan were discussed.

> **Give facts of ER's contacts with EE about this interview. State what EE has said about his willingness to cooperate in the interview. If contact was more than a few minutes, describe how much of the content planned for the interview was discussed.**

B. FORMULATION OF THE PROBLEM

1. *Description of the problem.* From past knowledge, ER believes EE has persistently failed to accomplish meaningful goals academically and vocationally. ER is interested in helping EE analyze the forces which maintain EE in his present pattern of behavior, and evaluating what EE may wish to do to change the situation.

> **Describe the nature of the problem that creates the need for an interview. Training interviews are usually limited to getting EE's perceptions of his situation and EE's ideas of what causes the problem.**

2. *Information available.* EE has held and been fired from (or quit) six manual labor jobs in the last six months. From contacts with relatives, ER believes EE still owes money to numerous friends, relatives, and creditors. It is rumored by his relatives that he has written several bad checks. He has had several minor run-ins with the law, but he never has been arrested.

> **List all facts now known. Alleged facts should be so identified—including the sources of the information. Interviewing past acquaintances makes this portion espe-**

cially complex: much is usually known, but the sources may not be recalled to keep from invoking assumptions based on prior information, it is easiest for training purposes to interview a stranger.

C. OUTPUTS

Analyses, conclusions, or decisions to be made from the data collected from EE.

Specify here the uses to be made of the data collected.

The report. Since this is a voluntary interview to give ER practice, the report is to be directed to the instructor who will be the only person to read it. It will not be shown to EE.

For training interviews, the ethical handling of the data and report should be specified. For on-the-job training, the report may be used in the usual ways by the organization. The report should be countersigned by the person supervising the on-the-job training.

1. *Descripion of EE's self-concept* (output 1). How he perceives his present pattern of behavior; what his goals are; what he thinks prevents/helps him reach his goals.

This output contains the analysis of EE's own perceptions of his present situation, his goals, and what he thinks causes his failures and successes. ER will be expected only to summarize what EE has said, not make inferences beyond the data obtained.

2. *Prognosis of EE's future behavior* (output 2). How likely is he to change? How does he think he will cope with the problems he has not yet resolved?

Again, this output deals only with a summary of EE's own opinions about his prognosis.

D. EE INPUTS

Data needed from EE to accomplish the intended outputs.

Itemize the information that should yield an accurate summary of the two planned outputs.

1. *EE's description of his present situation.* **(These data relate to output 1.)**
   a. Work
   b. Finances
   c. Personal adjustment
   d. Social relationships
   e. Relations with relatives

2. *EE's perceptions of the effects of his present situation on himself.* **(For output 1.)**
   a. What satisfactions/dissatisfactions does he now experience?
   b. What does he see as the reasons or causes of the satisfactions/dissatisfactions he now experiences?
   c. How does he react emotionally to his usual pattern of functioning?

3. *EE's description and explanation of his goals.* **(For output 1.)**
   a. What are his immediate goals?
   b. What are his long-term goals?
   c. What does he think helps him reach his goals?
   d. What does he think hinders him in reaching his goals?
   e. How much help/hindrance does he attribute to others?
   f. How much help/hindrance does he attribute to his own efforts?

4. *EE's evaluation of his potential for reaching his goals.* **(For output 2.)**
   a. What does he think would have to change in himself?
   b. What does he think would have to change in others?
   c. How likely does he think others are to change himself?
   d. How likely does he think others are to change?

QUESTIONS TRAINEES ASK ABOUT THE INTERVIEW PLAN

Writing up your first plan may be tedious. Planning comes much easier with practice. Here are some of the questions trainees usually ask, and some suggestions about how to proceed.

1. *Shouldn't I depict the professional role I intend to take in real life? (from a student in college)*

Answer. No. You'll learn more by depicting exactly what your present role is. Aside from avoiding confusion in your critique of the interview, it is also ethically incorrect to represent yourself to EE or even in the write-up as more qualified than you are.

2. *It's easier for me to get a friend to volunteer. Why use a stranger? (from a student in college)*

Answer. You already think you know a lot about your friend. You will tend to skip over important questions you should ask, and impose your assumptions on your friend. Also, your friend is likely to assume you already understand him. So using a friend is actually more artificial than using a stranger. In terms of the relational issues, you already have a pattern of interacting established with your friend. You'll learn more by beginning fresh with a stranger—it's easier to see what's happening in a brand new relationship.

3. *Is it all right to use an actual interview for on-the-job training?*

Answer. Certainly. The only source of confusion is in those roles where you, as ER, are expected to do more than gather information. In many instances, ER is expected to *give* information too. For example, in professional recruiting, the employment interviewer may spend a large portion of the interview giving information about the employing organization. In fact, research on the employment interview shows that ERs talk more than EEs; see Mayfield (1964). In a state employment agency, the placement interviewer may be expected to diagnose training needs and give advice. For purposes of depth interviewing training, the first interview you select should be limited to getting information about EE.

4. *Experienced interviewers don't use a written plan. Why should I?*

Answer. To handle well the logical issues in interviewing, developing planning habits is essential. To plan is to take an intellectual risk. You, as most people, probably avoid such risk-taking when possible. Skillful experienced interviewers always have an implicit plan. Their skill level is evident in how thorough and communicative their reports are. After writing up a few plans, you'll have similar skills.

5. *What right do I have to invade the privacy of a volunteer EE?*

Answer. You have no right, except by the volunteer EE's consent. Further, by assuring complete confidentiality and anonymity of the tape recording and the report, you are responsible for the professional ethics in the relationship. If a potential EE is unsure about being willing to reveal personal information in a practice interview, get a different volunteer. If a volunteer EE appears quite willing, but you are still hesitant, watch for your own inhibitions interfering with your training—some students are oversensitive to the slightest nonverbal cue from volunteer EEs that the interview is getting "too personal."

6. *Does there have to be a "problem" to have a useful interview?*

Answer. No. You should be certain, however, that EE has had some kind of intense personal experience—the more recent, the better he can recall it—he is willing to discuss. The "problem" orientation often proves useful because personal feelings are more accessible when a person is still in the process of working out a problem situation. Once resolved, the natural tendency is to suppress or repress the kind and degree of feelings originally involved.

7. *Why state the outputs? Aren't they obvious?*

Answer. The outputs may seem obvious. It is amazing, however, to see the gross inadequacies of some professional reports. They do not answer questions of concern to others in the organization. They may dwell at length on topics of interest only to the interviewer. (For example, a clinical psychologist may write pages on Freudian dynamics in a report to a rehabilitation counselor who wants to know the practical limits imposed on a person's vocational potential!) They may try to answer questions in an interview that are more efficiently or validly answered by some other source of information (for example, financial integrity is best determined by credit reports; intelligence is best estimated by standardized intelligence tests; physical health is best diagnosed by a physician). In short, defining the outputs assures that ER will use the interview as efficiently and validly as possible. Most authors agree that a moderate to high structure is the most promising. (See entries for this chapter in the Annotated Bibliography.) For example, consider the wide range of outputs that may relate to a diagnostic interview by a psychiatrist in a mental hospital, such as the following:

☐ Determine if any special security is needed.
☐ Recommend best possible placement in the hospital. With which staff and patient group will the patient best function?
☐ Personality analysis: explanation and prediction of behaviors.
☐ Interpersonal system analysis: how the personality dynamics interrelated in the particular social systems in which the patient has been functioning.
☐ Recommend immediate and long-term therapy.
☐ Recommend length of hospital stay, possible placement after discharge.

8. *How do I go about developing EE inputs?*

Answer. Beginning with each output, imagine the experiences EE may have had that might give you relevant information. In the training interview, making up the list of needed data is much simplified by the limitation that you only are seeking EE's *perceptions* of his past experiences, present difficulties, and future hopes. You are not expected to make broad inferences beyond the data you collect about EE's perceptions.

9. *Can one input connect with more than one output?*

Answer. Yes, especially when EE gives you a long descriptive answer to a question. To make a single EE input of use for more than one output, however, some probing is usually necessary. For example, in an employment interview, the work history of the applicant may pertain to several outputs: (a) evaluation of stability of motivation to work; (b) analysis of interpersonal skills in working with peers and superiors; (c) analysis of applicant's self-concept in terms of strengths and weaknesses.

10. *How do I know what specific questions to ask EE?*

Answer. If you feel unsure of how to get started, write out the wording of questions for each item on your EE inputs. Here are some examples from those given under input 1 of the interview plan.

Plan	Question
1. Jim's description of his present situation.	
a. Work	I'd like you to tell me about what you are now doing, both at work and in your personal and social relationships. Let's begin with your work. Tell me about the work you are doing now.
b. Finances	Next I'd like to know about how you handle your personal finances. Tell me about your income, your regular expenses, and any financial difficulties you may be having.
c. Personal living arrangements	Would you describe your present living arrangements?
d. Social relationships	What are the regular social relationships you have?
e. Relations with relatives	With which of your relatives do you now have regular contact?

11. *Is a list of specific questions always useful?*

Answer. No. After one or two practice interviews, you will no longer need an interview schedule, except in research studies in which the wording of questions must remain the same. You will quickly develop the ability spontaneously to generate questions from your planned input and, at the same time, flow smoothly from the cues EE gives you.

12. *How do I tell if my plan is coherent and extensive enough?*

Answer. After you have made the first draft, put it aside for a few hours or a day. Then take each input needed and match it against the related output(s). It is helpful to use a blackboard or a large sheet of paper and write out the outputs in one column with the related inputs in a parallel column. After jotting down all the items from your planned outputs and inputs, inspect them for the following:

(a) Are some of your planned inputs related to so many (two or more) outputs that it would be difficult to judge how to use them? If so, this means you should break the one planned input down into more specific items which relate to just one planned output.

(b) Assuming your planned inputs are pertinent, evaluate the wording of each related output. Sometimes outputs are worded so vaguely that *no* inputs would help ER to draw conclusions! For example, consider this planned output: "A prognosis of EE's future behavior and the likelihood of change." This wording is too vague and too broad. To be workable, the output should be reworded to state what specific future behavior and what direction of change are to be predicted.

(c) Now look over each output and the group of related inputs. See if all aspects of the output are adequately covered by the related inputs. A potentially productive topic may be overlooked in the first draft.

In summary, trainees have found that writing up a plan

☐ Helps ER organize his thoughts before conducting the interview.

☐ Helps generate a list of specific questions, if needed.

☐ Serves as a general guide throughout the interview, especially on how to begin with an explanation of the purpose and introduction of the topics to be covered.

☐ Prevents ER from jumping to conclusions without adequate information from EE.

In Chapter 6, you will see the essential value of the plan as you critique the adequacy of the data you have obtained in a practice interview. The outline in the plan serves as the criteria for the content you should have covered. The plan also is essential in part of the critique of the logical and relational processes of the interview (this is explained in Chapter 9).

We turn next to setting up your first practice interview.

5

HOW TO SET UP, CONDUCT, AND TRANSCRIBE A PRACTICE INTERVIEW

You have learned what is to be included in an interview plan. In this chapter you will learn, step by step, what to do to prepare for your first practice interview, how to conduct it, and what precautions to take so you will be ready to complete a thorough critique of your interviewing skills.

Step 1. Select EE. If you are a student, you have a wide latitude of choice. Best results are obtained by interviewing strangers whose roles are quite different from yours. Students have successfully recruited EEs from homes for the aged, juvenile detention homes, poverty program participants, and friends who know others in unusual circumstances (such as unwed mothers). If you are doing on-the-job training, remember the precautions given in the last chapter: try to set up your first practice interview so that your sole purpose is getting information from EE.

Step 2. Preliminary visit with EE. It is helpful to have a five to ten minute visit with the potential EE. You should explain the special nature of this practice interview, which includes explaining the confidential nature of the audio or video recording and the report and how EE's personal identity will be protected. A student ER protects EE's identity by using a pseudonym in the transcript and analysis; the instructor does not know

EE's real name. Further, no one, including the instructor, should be allowed to listen to or see the tape without specific approval from EE. If ER is an on-the-job trainee, EE is assured that ER's supervisor will review the interview procedure and the conclusions drawn by ER so that improper judgments will not be made by ER; EE's identity, of course, is not normally protected, except that the usual confidential channels inside the organization would be followed. During the preliminary visit, also discuss with EE the general nature of the topic you think would be interesting. Do not go into detail with EE at this time. The goal here is to get EE's general agreement that the topic is of interest to him and that he is willing to discuss it under the confidential conditions you have explained. If EE appears reluctant, thank him for his time and pick another possible EE.

Step 3. Prepare the plan, as explained in Chapter 4. If needed, prepare a list of questions.

Step 4. Schedule a time and place for the interview, if you haven't already done so. Be sure you have an audio or video tape recorder available at that time. In advance, be sure you know how to record on the specific type of recorder you intend to use. Trainees have a surprising rate of failure in recording their first interviews. Secure enough tape to record for at least half an hour. Ask an experienced person if you have any doubts about how to use the recorder. Practice turning it on and off until you can do it with ease. Unfamiliarity with the recorder makes you very tense at the start of your first interview! Make sure the equipment *is "now"* recording before EE arrives.

Step 5. Conduct the interview. There are three essential parts to cover at the beginning of the interview.

1. Restate the purpose and ethics. Remind EE that this is a practice interview, for your benefit, and that his identity will be protected.
2. State the scope of the topics to be covered. Give EE an overview of what you hope to obtain from him.
3. Begin the first topic by establishing an informational base.

Ask descriptive questions first—for example, "Tell me about the vocational training you have had."

You will find that this approach to beginning an interview is the most efficient way to establish rapport and a framework for probing later in the interview. (The role-play in Chapter 3 on starting an interview may have helped.) The descriptive question builds rapport for two reasons. Asking a broad question indicates that you trust EE to give you a meaningful answer. And it asks primarily for factual information—the easiest type of answer for EE to give. The descriptive question also provides the essential framework for later probing: you must know the particulars of EE's experience—say, at work—before you can understand his opinions and feelings. Each time you begin a new topic, start with an informational base. Inexperienced interviewers tend to jump into opinion or feeling questions without having established a clear, mutual picture with EE of the facts of the situation. Below are examples of beginnings of interviews. See what you think of how ER is doing. A critique is given in the right-hand column.

Interview with Susan Spike	*Critique*
ER: This interview is going to be for my own purposes of learning how to do interviews and how to establish rapport with an interviewee. And, I'd like to explore what you think about yourself as an area of major interest, and, to start off with, why don't you give me a brief sketch of your present situation and . . . are you in school now?	A good start for explaining the purpose. Does not remind EE of the ethics of the interview. Too brief a sketch of the overall topic—"yourself" is too vague. Should explain more of what ER wants to know about EE's present situation. Ending with a "yes-no" question leaves little room for EE to comment.

Interview with Carl Crown	Critique
EE: Nobody's going to know who this is, will they?	
ER: . . . No, no . . . This will be completely anonymous, and your name will be disguised completely.	ER correctly deals with EE's first expression of concern. The ethical provision for anonymity is well covered.
EE: *(Laughs)* All right . . .	EE is perhaps showing some relief of his tension by laughing.
ER: The only person to see the verbatim transcript of the tape will be the teacher, and he's . . .	ER interrupts EE to continue his explanation of the ethics. The assurance would be more convincing if ER were more relaxed so he did not interrupt EE.
EE: You won't play it in the class, will you?	
ER: No, no. That never happens . . . Uh umm.	An additional important guarantee of ER's confidentiality is given.
EE: Okay . . . *(Laughs)* I'm getting more scared all the time. . .	EE tells ER directly that he is not convinced by the assurances.
ER: *(Laughs with EE)* Oh . . . well, I assure you . . . there's nothing to worry about . . . we're not going to take you apart or anything.	ER is groping awkwardly here to try to respond to EE's feelings. Would have been better to ask "What is it that makes you so scared?"
EE: There's not much to take apart . . . *(Almost in a whisper)*	EE is expressing very tender, frightful feelings about himself, posing a problem to ER: shift to intended beginning of the interview, and try to complete the introduction, or pick up

ER: Well . . . first of all, let's just sort of start at the top of your current situation . . . maybe review a little bit . . . if that's alright . . . right now you're in real estate school . . .

with the feelings EE is emitting.

ER decides to try to start with his first planned question. He has not reviewed the purpose of the interview. He has not been able to sketch out the scope of the topic of the interview. The wording of his first question leaves EE with the option of answering only "yes" or "no." Most important, ER does not indicate to EE what he intends to do about the feelings EE has just expressed, leaving EE feeling cut off.

Interview with Dave Downs	*Critique*
ER: Okay now. Well, uh, I wanted to thank you for coming up here, for offering to do this interview.	Good start with a "thank you" to build rapport.
EE: Umm. Uh huh.	
ER: Uh, as I mentioned before, this is only a practice interview . . . a practice interview on my part . . .	
EE: Okay . . .	EE interrupts, perhaps to reassure ER.
ER: I'm doing this as a, to fill a requirement for one of the courses at the university. I wanted to as-	ER explains purpose, perhaps too briefly for EE to understand what will be done with the transcript and tape in terms

sure you once more that anything that's said here will be held in strictest confidence. And the only other person besides you and me who will see this, uh transcript will be the uh, professor of the course.

of their utility for ER's training. Begins to explain the ethics of the interview.

EE: Uh huh.

ER: And, uh, even then, I'll use a false name, a pseudonym, for you so he won't, there'll be no way that he'll be able to connect this back . . .

ER finishes explanation of the ethics.

EE: Okay . . .

EE is expressing agreement to help.

ER: . . . to you. Uh, to go over briefly the points that I wanted to cover in this interview which we discussed earlier, uh, I wanted to talk about the, this experience, this emotional experience that you had, I believe, a couple weeks ago.

ER begins to explain the topic.

EE: Uh huh.

ER: Uh, sort of a near nervous breakdown. Uh, how it affected you, what caused it, how you overcame it, and uh, whether it left any lasting effects on your, oh, say goals.

ER manages to complete the overview of the topic. While a bit nervous with the hesitancies shown by the "uhs," ER nevertheless adequately structures the topic.

EE: Yes.	
ER: So, first of all, do you want to, uh, say describe the events immediately leading up to this experience?	ER completes the introduction well by asking a clearly-worded, open-ended, factual descriptive question.

The three sample interviews show progressively increasing adequacy in covering the suggested components of the introduction of the interview. The interview with Susan Spike had too brief an introduction and ended with a closed-ended beginning question. The interview with Carl Crown put ER somewhat off guard because EE initiated the first question about confidentiality and suddenly exposed his fear. ER first tried intellectually to reassure EE about his concerns; failing to do so, ER shifted to a too-brief introduction and, as in the Susan Spike interview, ended with a closed beginning question. The more adequate third interview with Dave Downs demonstrates thorough coverage of the purpose, sketch of the topic, and beginning descriptive factual question, although ER was a bit nervous.

Step 6. End the interview. After you have fairly well covered the scope you intended, close off the interview by summing up the main points you have obtained from EE. Express your appreciation for his cooperation. Ask him if he has any questions about what you are going to do next. Agree to show him the transcript, not the analysis. He may want to listen to the tape; you are obliged to accede to this request. Be careful not to cut off EE if he is at an emotional high point. Wait a few minutes before ending.

Step 7. Transcribe the tape. Using only the right-hand half of your paper, transcribe the tape. Number each ER and EE input sequentially. Here is an example. (A completed transcript of an interview appears in the Appendix.)

EE: (*pseudonym*)
ER: (*name*)
Date:

Input number	Speaker	Input
1.	ER:	Jim, this is just a demonstration interview on my part. I am doing this as an assignment for a class. We're required to interview someone, and it's practice for us in asking questions and analyzing our style.
(*Double space between speakers.*)		
2.	EE:	Okay.
3.	ER:	What are you doing right now? Are you working?
4.	EE:	Yeh, I'm working out in Somersville.

For greater speed, run just a few words on the tape, stop it, write them down, then another few words. Listening to an entire sentence or more is less efficient; you will usually have to rewind the tape to get all the words. After your first rough draft, go back over the tape to be sure you have all the audible words and non-verbal sounds recorded. Using videotape, also take notes on other ER and EE nonverbal patterns. Before you begin transcribing, review Chapters 3 and 7 so you will know all the nonverbal items to include. From the first draft, type up at least two copies (a third is sometimes handy) of the transcript. Remember to use only the right-hand half of the page.

When your transcript is typed, you are ready to analyze the manifest content. Turn to Chapter 6.

6

HOW TO ANALYZE THE MANIFEST CONTENT OF AN INTERVIEW

You have already begun to evaluate your practice interview as you have listened to or viewed your tape and transcribed it. You have felt good about some parts of it. You have seen some parts that could have been done better. Now you are ready for a more systematic analysis and evaluation of your interview. Chapters 6 through 9 show you how to do a systematic evaluation of the content you obtained and the interactional processes that occurred. In this chapter, you will learn how to summarize and evaluate the information EE has given you. This is a critique of the manifest content you actually obtained, compared with the information your plan called for you to obtain. In Chapters 7 through 9, you will learn how to categorize and evaluate the latent content in terms of the interpersonal processes of the logical and relational issues outlined in Chapters 1, 2, and 3.

ANALYSIS OF MANIFEST CONTENT OF EE INPUTS

In this chapter, you will learn how to summarize EE's actual inputs, how to formulate the amalgamated summaries of your planned outputs, and how to critique the adequacy of the inputs you obtained from EE. We are interested in these questions:

◻ For each planned input, how much information did you get?

How adequate is the information you did obtain? That is, how thoroughly did you cover the topic?

What new inputs did you introduce?

What output conclusions can you make? How well documented are they from obtained inputs? *(what are based on?)*

The steps below guide you through the analysis of the manifest content of the EE inputs.

Step 1. Get the list of your planned inputs (numbered 1a, 1b, 1c, 2a, 2b, 2c, and so forth). Using the second (carbon) copy of the typed transcript, connect each ER question-EE statement pair with the relevant planned input(s). Write in the planned input number to the right of each EE statement on the transcript. Your working copy will look like this, using a small portion of the interview with Jim Smith:

look at P 50.

Input number	Speaker	Input	Planned input number
3	ER:	What are you doing right now? Are you working?	
4	EE:	Yeh, I'm working out in Somersville.	1a (present work situation)
5	ER:	What kind of work is it?	
6	EE:	Well, it's in a onion shed. I'm foreman of a crew in charge of loading trucks and boxcars.	1a
7	ER:	What kind of hours do you work?	
8	EE:	God-awful hours. (*Laughter*) I usually work about 10 to 12 hours a day.	2b (dissatisfaction EE experiences)

17	ER:	What other kinds of work have you done?	
18	EE:	Oh, I've . . . I started out driving tractor, and then I worked in a lumber mill [*etc.*].	5a (new; past work experience)

(*When a new topic is introduced, assign it a new topic number, as above, and add the topic title at the end of your original list of planned inputs. In the Jim Smith interview, four new topics were introduced. (See the complete analysis in the Appendix, Section III.)*)

47	ER:	Do you owe other debts?	
48	EE:	Well, outside of some back rent, no. And, well, back rent and a few bad checks (*laughs*). I, ah, I'm not that actually far behind right now. It's just that I can't stop. I mean, it's enough if I stop working and went to school, I'd never make it. I couldn't make enough money to pay for it.	1b (present financial situation) 3d (what hinders present goals)

(*This is an example of how one EE statement may relate to two (or more) of the planned inputs. Simply show both planned input numbers.*)

Continue this procedure through the entire transcript. You do not need to recheck your work at this point. You will recheck your work in an easier way in step 3.

Step 2. Cut up the transcript into each ER question-EE statement pair. Be careful to include the relevant preceding ER question with the EE response. After cutting up one copy of the entire transcript, sort each pair of inputs into piles for each topic. If an EE input relates to several topics, put it first in the topic with the lowest topical number. After dealing with a multiple-numbered input on the first topic, move it to the next pile.

Step 3. Scan through the pile of EE inputs on the first topic.

You may find some inputs that do not belong. Relocate them in the correct topical pile. You may recall other inputs that should be in the pile for the first topic. Relocate them. Next, order the EE inputs on the first topic in a sequence that is meaningful to you. In some instances, there may be two or more subthemes.

Step 4. Record your manifest content analysis according to the following instructions (given in boldface type below the sample format):

Jim's description of his present work situation (input 1a)
 Title the topic.
1. *EE inputs.* 4, 6, 122, 124.
  List all EE input numbers you think are related to this topic. Include EE input numbers that appear to give duplicate information.
2. *Summary.* Jim says he is now a foreman (6) over two or three men (124) in charge of loading trucks and boxcars in an onion shed (6) in Somersville (4). He is responsible for seeing that trucks are loaded as promptly as possible, upon being told by his boss when a truck is due (122).
  Having arranged the inputs in some logical sequence in step 3, condense the information into easily readable sentences. After each summary phrase, show in parentheses the EE input number from which the information was taken.
3. *Evaluation.* The four EE inputs about Jim's present work situation identitfy the location and Jim's general responsibilities. We do not know (a) how long he has been working there; (b) how Jim reacts to specific conditions on the job; (c) what kind of relationship Jim has with his boss. With this much data missing, little can be inferred for the output.
  Evaluate how adequately you have covered the scope of the topic. What did you find out as shown in the summary? (Don't repeat the summary here.) What other information would you need to give a complete picture? List the other information needed.

From the list of data needed, judge how useful the obtained inputs will be for drawing conclusions in the output formulation.

See additional examples on pp. 138–145. Perform the same analysis of each planned topic and each new topic introduced during the interview.

HOW TO FORMULATE OUTPUTS

With a summary and an evaluation of the EE inputs on each topic, you are now prepared to condense your report into some statements of output. Here are the steps.

Step 1. Review all summaries and evaluations. Pencil by each one the output numbers they relate to. For any topic on which no data or most data needed are missing, write "SKIP."

Step 2. For the first output topic, record your EE input analysis according to the following instructions:

Jim's self-concept (ouput 1)
    Title the topic.
1. *EE input topics.* 1c, 2a, 2b, 3a, 3c, 3d, 3f.
    List all EE input topic numbers you think are related to this output. Exclude input topic numbers you have marked "SKIP."
2. *Findings.* Jim has a very negative self-concept: "dumb, stupid, ignorant, a clod, lazy, cowardly" are the words he uses (1c). He finds himself very weak in solving his problems. He tends to blame others, laugh them off, and remain preoccupied with his immediate gratifications (1c). His self-concept is so negative he says he cannot accept feedback from others about his qualities (1c). He does not appear to be gaining strong positive rewards from his present pattern of behavior (he calls it "growing up" or "sowing wild oats") (2a), but is swept along by the incentives of his immediate goals (2b). He finds he has great difficulty getting started on his problems and long-term goals (2b). In the

distant future are "normal" goals of marriage and a real home (3b). He thinks a new job that may open up next month will be a change for the better, but he has little concept of how to advance except by working harder than others (3a, 3c). Jim is so preoccupied with his immediate goals he cannot get started on longer-term goals (3d). He realizes he was unreliable in the past at work, but says he now goes to work even if he does not want to (3f). He believes he really is intelligent, but does not use his ability (1c, 3f).

> **Condense related EE input topical summaries. Compose summary themes, showing topics from which each theme is taken, in parentheses. Avoid terminology not used in input summaries. Do not make broad inferences that cannot be directly traced to topical summaries. (This book stops with this first intellectual step in formulating output conclusions. Additional inferential steps are discussed in Levy, 1963 and Sundberg and Tyler; 1962.)**

3. *Evaluation.* The above conclusions appear to be adequately documented in the interview. Data were inadequate on planned topics 1b (finances), 1d (social relationships), 1e (relations with relatives), 3e (help/hindrance from others), and 4b (changes in others). On topics 2a, 2b, 3b, 3c, 3d, 3f, 4a, and 4c data were adequate in terms of descriptions of Jim's internal emotional states, but were inadequate in terms of how Jim actually sees himself functioning interpersonally. We do not know the degree to which Jim's actual functioning may alter as he interacts with others.

> **State how adequately the findings are documented in the interview. List topics on which no data or inadequate data were obtained. List topics for which some data were usable, but also needed more information. Summarize the topical areas for which more information is needed.**

See additional examples on p. 146. Perform the same analysis of each planned output topic.

You have now completed a critique of how well you dealt with the planned versus actual coverage of topics in the interview. Typically, ERs are optimistic before and somewhat depressed after doing the manifest content analysis of their first practice interview. Surely, to have a volunteer EE give many answers to the series of questions you managed to conjur up is encouraging. This makes ER feel optimistic. But with systematic summary and evaluation of each topic, the missing parts begin to show up. The fact that volunteer EEs tend to allow ER to control the interview, or at least produce many responses, momentarily clouds the question of the adequacy of the information being obtained. It is almost as if ER is saying to himself during the interview: "Boy! I got EE to say something on that planned topic, so I'll go on to the next topic!" The depression or frustration you may be experiencing is to be expected. No one likes to feel good about a task he has done, only to learn later that he did not do so well.

Compare your performance with other beginning ERs'. If you wrote "SKIP" on less than one-third of your planned topics, you have done better than the typical novice. If you wrote "SKIP" on one-third or more of your planned topics, you have done about the same as the typical trainee. In the Jim Smith interview (Section III in the Appendix) there are six SKIPS out of eighteen preplanned topics. Hence the performance of this ER also was "average."

Give yourself credit for introducing relevant new topics—even if the data were inadequate to use in the outputs. The fact that you were alert and flexible enough to ask unanticipated questions is a crucial skill for interviewing.

7

HOW TO CATEGORIZE INPUTS FOR PROCESS ANALYSIS

You are ready to begin the process analysis of your interview. In the manifest analysis we were concerned with the adequacy of the information obtained from EE. Now the focus shifts to latent content in the interactions of ER and EE: "How did ER and EE handle the process, logically and relationally?"

There are three steps in this analysis. First, in this chapter, you will learn how to categorize the communication in each ER and EE input. Second, in Chapter 8, you will learn how to identify and analyze the key points of interaction in the interview—the parts of the interview where you were most aware of the logical and relational issues. Third, in Chapter 9, you will learn how to use the results of the input categorization and the interaction analysis to critique your interviewing skills, including how well you asked questions, the response patterns of the EE, how well you probed, how you and EE paced the interview, the impact of nonverbal ER and EE communications, and the rapport developed.

In this chapter, input categories are described and questions students commonly ask about the coding are answered. You categorize inputs so you can see the patterns of interaction in the interview. For example, if you asked EE a question calling for an opinion response, what kind of answer did you actually get—facts, opinions, and/or feelings? As you code the categories for each input, and review the results, you will begin to apprehend a pattern of interaction which shows how logical and relational issues were handled by both you and EE.

Below are the input categories you use for labeling each ER and EE question, statement, and nonverbal behavior.

ER main question	Definition	Examples
FACT Q	*Factual* Q. Asks for factual information. Time perspective: past or present. Include questions of *past opinion* and *past feelings*.	"When were you born?" "Did you formerly believe in nonviolence?" "How were you feeling yesterday?"
OPIN Q	*Opinion* Q. Asks for EE's beliefs, attitudes, or values. Time perspective: present or future. This also includes questions of how EE thinks he may *feel* in the future.	"What do you think causes race riots?" "Do you think your education will help you get a job?" "Do you think you'll still feel happy tomorrow?"
DESC Q	*Descriptive* Q. Asks for a narrative account of an experience or situation, including implied FACT, OPIN, and FEEL Q. Time perspective: past or present.	"Tell me about your family."
FEEL Q*	*Feeling* Q. Asks for the pres-	"What are your pres-

---

* This narrow definition implies the training goal of getting ER and EE to focus on the here-and-now affect, as emphasized by the theoretical orientation of this book. See Chapters 1 and 2.

ent inner emotional state of EE. Time perspective: *present* only. (Not future: see OPIN Q, SUP Q; not past: see FACT Q.)

ent reactions to the conflict you experience with your father?"

ER special-purpose question	*Definition*	*Examples*
KNOW Q	*Knowledge* Q. Intended to evaluate EE's competence in a specific area of knowledge or skill.	"What have you found to be the best way to solve that kind of problem?"
PROBE (FACT)	*Probing* Q. A question following up a previous Q in which more factual information is requested.	"When did you say you had the accident?"
PROBE (OPIN)	Asks for more opinions, or to expand on EE's prior statement of OPIN.	"Tell me more exactly why you think the lower class should be taxed less."
PROBE (FEEL)	Asks for more explicit statement of EE's present inner emotional state.	"How did you actually *feel*, inside, when you found out you had failed math?"
LEAD (UNINF)	*Uninformed leading* Q. Asks question in form that implies ER already knows answer. Uninformed means ER had no way (before or during interview) to know the answer.	"You liked your Mother, didn't you?"
LEAD (INF)	*Informed leading* Q. Asks question in form that implies ER already knows an an-	"You are now 21 years old, aren't you?"

swer. Informed means ER had some way (before or during interview) to know the answer.

SUP Q	*Suppositional* Q. Asks EE how he might think, feel, or act in a hypothetical situation.	"Let's suppose you were hit by a close friend—what would you do?"
PROJ Q	*Projective* Q. Seeks information about EE's personality by asking indirectly in form of EE's OPIN or FEEL about another person.	"What kind of a boss was he?"
CR EX Q	*Cross-examination* Q. Repeats essentially same Q EE has already answered. Implies ER disbelieves EE.	(Usually used with FACT Q and OPIN Q.)
CF Q	*Clarification* Q. ER restates previous Q, implying EE did not give answer ER expected.	"What I meant was, . . .?"
DBL BAR Q	*Double barreled* Q. Asks two or more questions before EE has a chance to answer the first question. (Caused by ER anxiety.)	"When did you first notice you were getting depressed? Was it before or after you left home?"
	Also score DBL BAR Q even if first Q is incomplete.	"When did you . . . Were you depressed before or after you left home?"

EE may also ask any of the questions usually posed by ER.

ER statement Description

TOPIC	Explanation of topic(s) to be discussed in the interview.

PUR   *Purpose.* Explanation of ER's intent, or goal, in the interview.

RAP   *Rapport.* Small talk for secondary purpose such as warm-up at beginning of interview, or easing off at end of interview.

UN   *Unrelated narrative.* Comments unnecessary for the interview.

ECHO   *Echoing* what EE has already said; repeating almost verbatim.

ENC   *Encouragements.* Short comments which indicate ER's attentiveness to what EE is saying. May occur during EE's responses, but not have effect of interrupting—e.g., "I see," "Uh huh."

NV   *Nonverbal* expression such as a laugh, a sigh, a cough, clearing the throat, etc.

GUG*   *Guggle.* A short, usually staccato sound, such as "Ah" indicating the "guggler" may interrupt.

I   *Interruption.* Breaking into the middle of the other's statement, with a complete sentence or more.

ANT   *Anticipation.* Speaker guesses what other person is about to say, usually in an interrupting way.

AS   *Assumptive statement.* Speaker infers something not yet stated by other person. Similar to LEAD (UNINF) Q—e.g., "You know that most adolescents have hang-ups with authority figures." Similar to ADV, but usually a generalization.

ADV   *Advice-giving.* Suggests specific solution to problem presented by EE. "Have you tried organizing your schedule so you can study better?"

---

* The term "guggles" is taken from Richardson, Dohrenwend, and Klein (1965).

AGR	*Agreement*. ER states he agrees with what EE has said.
DISAGR	*Disagreement*. ER states he disagrees with what EE has said.
REFL	*Reflecting*. Nondirective method of feeding back to EE what he seems to be feeling. Used primarily for focusing on FEEL.
SUM	*Summarizing*. Nondirective method of feeding back to EE what he has stated, primarily in FACT and OPIN statements; may also include FEEL.

EE statement	Description
(Use same rules as for analogous question.)	
FACT	A specific bit of information.
OPIN	An *opinion;* either a belief, value, or attitude. Focused on an *external* object—e.g., "That teacher is incompetent."
DESC	A narrative account of an experience or situation, including FACT, OPIN, and FEEL statements.
FEEL	Description of the affective, *inner* state—e.g., "I feel indifferent and withdrawn when I am in that teacher's lecture."
KNOW	Statement of specialized *knowledge* or skill.
CFS	Clarification of former statement. Usually comes after ER's CF Q.
S	*Silence*, after ER has asked a question.

EE may also make any of the statements usually given by ER.

ER silence	Description
CS	*Courtesy silence*. ER pauses 2 to 4 seconds after

EE stops talking to allow EE time to think or add more, before asking another question.

PS   *Pregnant silence.* EE has failed to answer ER's question. ER then states more strongly what he wants from EE, and ER pauses 5 or more seconds —deliberately to put pressure on EE.

EE silence	Description
S	EE is silent a few seconds after ER has asked a question (except for PS above). Assign s to EE only for pauses up to 4 seconds and only when EE pauses after ER has spoken.

Using the Jim Smith interview, here are some examples of how categories are assigned. See pp. 118–120 for the content of the inputs.

Explanation	Category	Input number	Speaker
States ER's reason for doing the interview.	PUR	1	ER
EE indicates he agrees with ER's explanation of PUR.	AGR	2	EE
ER asks for factual information about EE's present activities. (Not scored DESC Q because ER did not indicate he wanted a narrative account of EE's present activities.)	FACT Q	3a	ER
A closed-ended question scored LEAD Q because the usual expectation of male adult is that he would be working. Scored (I) because ER knew in advance that EE was working as a day laborer.	LEAD (I) Q	3b	ER

Two questions are asked before EE has a chance to answer.	DBL BAR Q	3	ER
EE gives same factual information.	FACT	4	EE
ER is asking for more facts, and perhaps an opinion; "kind" is ambiguous to categorize.	DESC Q	5	RE
EE gives more factual information.	FACT	6	EE
ER again uses the ambiguous "kind." Scored FACT Q because hours worked inclines the intent of the question toward a fact rather than an opinion.	FACT Q	7	ER
Scored OPIN because EE is expressing an attitude (with emotional overtones) toward an object: the hours he says he works.	OPIN	8a	EE
Audible laughter is scored NV.	NV	8b	EE
Another bit of factual information.	FACT	8c	EE
"Like" connotes feelings, but ER asks for an attitude about an object—EE's work—hence scored OPIN.	OPIN Q	9	ER
Scored OPIN because prior question is scored OPIN.	OPIN	10	EE
The wording "Have you" forms a request for a factual report. (Might be misscored OPIN because ER's intent is to find out if EE's negative attitude has led him to think about looking for other types of work.) ER is using a FACT Q to get at an OPIN.	FACT	11	ER
"Yeah" is a report of a past action, hence a fact.	FACT	12	EE
ER's first open-ended OPIN Q. "Why" usually pulls for opinions, rather than facts or feelings.	OPIN Q	15	ER

". . . I don't care" implies a feeling but again (as in 10 above) EE is emitting an attitude about an external object—the people he works with.	OPIN	16	EE
A broader DESC Q.	DESC Q	17	ER
Scored DESC (FACT) rather than just FACT to reflect that EE has told a narrative (although brief) account of his past work.	DESC (FACT)	18	EE
Scored OPIN rather than FEEL for same reason as question 9 above.	OPIN Q	19	ER
EE's first FEEL; scored because it conveys an *inner reaction* in his experience. EE shows in NV laugh that he is *now* experiencing the feeling, or at least the aftermath of it.	FEEL	22a	EE
EE then briefly describes the story of what happened. Note both FACT and OPIN are included in the narrative. OPIN is scored for the phrase "you have to have 100 percent on your side or you don't go back" since this might or might not be accurate factually.	DESC (FACT, OPIN)	22b	EE
The first question is incomplete, but score DBL BAR Q.	OPIN Q, DBL BAR Q	23	ER
Scored AS because ER is invoking his opinion in the phrase "quite a few." Would be scored FACT if ER had merely stated the number of jobs.	AS	25b	ER
After a series of factual statements, in 28b, EE emits an opinion of himself, followed by a tense NV laugh. (Might be misscored FEEL because an affective state is implied.)	DESC (FACT, OPIN) NV	28b	EE

Now try your hand at categorizing your own transcript. Ask your instructor to review your judgments and make suggestions where you may be unclear. Here are some questions students frequently ask.

1. *Can more than one category be assigned to one input?*

Answer. Yes. The categories are not intended to be mutually exclusive.

2. *How can I tell if an EE response is* OPIN *or* FEEL?

Answer. OPIN focuses on an external object or person, but does imply EE's feelings. The problem is, without a direct expression of his feelings, ER doesn't know precisely what they are. FEEL describes an inner state (happy, sad, angry, elated, dejected, high, low, expansive, withdrawn, frustrated) which may or may not be connected with an external object or person. FEEL focuses on EE's *own* reactions; OPIN focuses on characteristics EE ascribes to other objects or persons. Further, FEEL is limited to experiences in the present tense only. OPIN may be present or future tense.

3. *When can I count a question as a probe?*

Answer. A probe is credited whenever ER uses a cue previously given by EE. The cue may be in an earlier portion of the interview, or it may be EE's last response.

4. *What is the difference between a* PROBE (FEEL) Q *and* REFL?

Answer. A PROBE (FEEL) Q usually refers to a hint just given by EE that he has a strong feeling of some kind. ER uses the PROBE (FEEL) Q to enable EE to express his feeling more directly. REFL, a nondirective counseling technique, usually involves an inference by ER of what EE feels; also, it usually involves several—often mixed—feelings. The probe pressures EE to express a feeling directly; it puts the burden on EE. The REFL puts the burden on ER to sense how EE is feeling: EE needs merely to agree or disagree that ER is correct. A successful REFL usually results in further, deeper emotional expression by EE.

5. *How can I tell the difference between* LEAD Qs *versus* FACT, FEEL, *and* OPIN Qs?

Answer. All LEAD Qs ask for fact, feeling, or opinion. In addition, all LEAD Qs are closed—they are answerable with one or a few words, and the answer ER expects is implied in the wording of the question. Most confusing to categorize is a PROBE vs. a LEAD (INF) Q. Score probe when possible—when a previous ER Q and EE cue are being followed up. When a new topic is introduced by ER, and it is closed-ended and the answer expected is hinted by the wording of ER's question, score either LEAD (UNINF) or LEAD (INF) Q.

6. *What is the difference between* LEAD (UNINF) *and* LEAD (INF) *Qs?*

Answer. Both types of LEAD Q hint that ER expects a certain answer, either by the content or the nonverbal cues he gives. The UNINF Q is scored when there is no prior information available to ER before or during the interview that would indicate what answer to expect. The prior information would show up in the outline of the plan. If any cue was given by EE earlier in the interview to suggest what answer to expect, score the question as LEAD (INF).

7. *What is the significance of a* LEAD (INF) *Q?*

Answer. The purpose of a LEAD (INF) Q is to ask EE to confirm a hunch ER has developed. If ER uses frequent LEAD (INF) Q, he may be showing anxiety about controlling the interview—that is, he is indicating to EE he does not want to give EE very much room to express himself. ER does not trust EE. Predictably, EE will become less trustworthy by being more brief in his answers, or vague; or EE will switch to creating and answering his *own* question! Richardson et al., 1965 provide a more complete discussion of this issue.*)

8. *What does it mean if ER frequently uses* LEAD (UNINF) *Q?*

Answer. It means ER is momentarily out of touch with the communications going on in the interview. It usually jolts EE and sometimes makes him angry. EE says to himself: "What the hell does he mean by that?" Take the LEAD (UNINF) Q as a sign of incompetence; try to eliminate them.

---

* See pp. 188–189.

9. *What makes a* SUP Q *different from a* FEEL Q? *Why use it?*

Answer. Both types of Q aim at EE's inner emotional state. FEEL Q is scored when ER asks directly for FEEL information from EE. A SUP Q is indirect because it asks about a hypothetical situation, either historically oriented or futuristic. The indirect SUP Q may be used when direct approaches fail to yield sufficient FEEL information from EE. Sometimes EE will feel freer to answer a hypothetical question. To complete the inquiry, a productive SUP Q would have to be followed up by additional direct FEEL QS.

10. *How can I tell when to score a* PROJ Q?

Answer. Like the SUP Q, a PROJ Q is indirect. A PROJ Q asks about another person—what he is like. Sometimes EEs are freer to answer this type of indirect Q than direct OPIN or FEEL QS. Sometimes ER uses PROJ Q to supplement or compare against how EE answers direct questions. People tend to be freer in answering direct questions about the pleasant aspects of their self-concepts. Unpleasant opinions and feelings may be more easily obtained by use of this type of projective device. To complete the inquiry, a productive PROJ Q would have to be followed up by additional direct OPIN and FEEL QS.

11. *What is the difference between a* CR EX Q *and a* CF Q?

Answer. When ER doubts a previous answer, ER uses a CR EX Q deliberately to put pressure on EE to confirm the answer. A CF Q is usually less deliberate and is an effort by ER to get EE to listen better to his previous questions. CF QS usually follow the misunderstood question. CR EX QS sometimes are preceded by other questions before the repetition of the question of interest to ER.

12. *What does a frequent occurrence of* CF Q *indicate?*

Answer. ER is unsure of where he is trying to go in the interview. As with the DBL BAR Q, he is tripping over his own words, groping for increased clarity so that EE will understand better what he wants.

13. *What does a frequent occurrence of* DBL BAR Q *indicate?*

Answer. See 12 above. In the DBL BAR Q, ER catches himself before he allows EE a chance to answer. Then ER asks two complete (or incomplete) questions. EE then is free to pick the question which is easier for him to answer. The function of the DBL BAR Q, then, is to let EE off the hook. Skilled ERs seldom ask DBL BAR QS.

14. *When is UN scored?*

Answer. Unrelated narrative is unintentional discussion by EE or ER of a topic not connected with the interview plan. Inexperienced ERs sometimes do UN to relieve pressure on themselves, or to fill in an awkward gap during the interview.

15. *Can any question or statement category be used for EE?*

Answer. Yes.

So much for some of the more difficult aspects of categorizing. You may find it helpful first to pencil in the categories on your transcript. Then review it (after leaving it alone for a while), and watch especially for incorrect set. Incorrect set is misuse of categories repeatedly through the transcript. The most common error in first using the categories is to give credit for FEEL Q and answers when OPIN or FACT are all that is in evidence. Note again the distinctions explained in the FEEL, OPIN, and FACT category definitions and the answers to questions 2, 5, and 9 above.

After you have rechecked your categorizing, you are ready to begin a systematic critique of ER and EE interactions. In the next chapter, you will learn how to identify and evaluate the most critical interactions in the interview.

<table>
<tr><td>

8

</td><td>

HOW TO ANALYZE THE CRITICAL INTERACTIONS

</td></tr>
</table>

In Chapter 7, you learned how to categorize each ER and EE input. Now you are ready to examine how you and EE interacted—the give-and-take between you and EE on the logical and relational issues. This chapter shows you how to analyze a few key interactions you believe you did skillfully—and some you think you did poorly. (A complete example of a write-up of critical interactions is given in Section IV of the Appendix.) Step-by-step instructions follow.

STEP-BY-STEP INSTRUCTIONS

Step 1. Scan the entire transcript. Circle the ER and EE inputs you believe are exemplary of good and poor interactions. Include the first several interchanges. Then pick about one interaction per page, or about one out of every ten to fifteen interchanges. An interaction is one ER input plus the next EE input. Focus your attention on just one pair of such inputs, not a series that might represent a phase (for example, introduction) of the interview.

Step 2. For the first interaction chosen, diagnose the particular logical and relational issues you think are involved. Here's an example from the Jim Smith interview.

Category	Input number	Speaker	Input	Commentary on critical interactions
PUR	1	ER:	Jim, this is just a demonstration interview on my part. I am doing this as an assignment for a class. We're required to interview someone and it's practice for us in asking questions and analyzing our style.	*Logical issue.* ER omitted ethics in discussion of PUR and omitted TOPIC. ER explained his goal, but failed to explain the confidentiality of the interview and the topical goals for the EE.
AGR	2	EE:	Okay.	EE agreed to be interviewed — an action issue. *Relational issue.* ER stressed his goal and forgot to mention EE's goals because ER was worried about EE's willingness to get into his "problem," and EE's commitment (inclusion) to the interview. EE, however, showed his willingness to proceed.

Explanation. To evaluate the first interaction, first determine the adequacy of ER's initial statement as part of the logical process. As explained in Chapter 3 ER should (a) review the purpose and ethics, (b) scan the general topic, and (c) begin with a broad DESC Q. In the example above, ER emphasized his goals and did not refer to either the ethical treatment of the interview data or the topic. Thus, analysis of the logical process shows that ER stressed his and ignored EE's goals! From the relational process we learn what, if any, ER and EE feelings accompanied this breakdown in the logical process. In this case, ER recalled that he had suspected that EE would refuse to reveal data about his "problem" of an irregular work record. Thus ER expected EE to be uncooperative and to feel not included in the interview. ER's failure to review EE's goals and anonymity may be taken as evidence of ER's lack of trust in EE. Remember the suggestions in Chapter 3 about cues to feelings in the relational process. You are looking for specific feelings and their possible connections with how you and EE felt about being involved in the interview, how you were reacting to the control process, and how much you liked or disliked each other.

Step 3. Go on to the next selected interaction. Here's another example.

Category	Input number	Speaker	Input	Commentary on critical interactions
FACT Q, LEAD (I) Q, DBL BAR Q	3	ER:	What are you doing right now? Are you working?	*Logical issue.* ER's LEAD (I) Q and DBL BAR Q show his confusion and anxiety over the relational issue seen in input 1. Note ER's failure to start with a broad DESC Q, further showing he does not trust EE to give informative answers.

Category	Input number	Speaker	Input	Commentary on critical interactions
FACT	4	EE:	Yeh, I'm working out in Somersville.	*Relational issue.* ER was also feeling unsure of how well he could control EE, having already lost some control by starting the interview incorrectly. Thus far, EE appeared at ease, and gave ER exactly the information asked for.

Explanation. Input 3 completes the introduction. Analysis of the logical issues shows poorly worded questions and failure to begin with a broad DESC Q. ER's expectation that EE would be uncooperative and uninformative is reflected in his use of a LEAD (I) Q, which was unnecessary because ER already had the information. The DBL BAR Q also indicates ER's lack of trust in EE and ER's confusion over how to get into the correct logical focus. Relationally, we see the control issue entering in, confounding the concern ER already had in input 1 over EE's commitment. Thus far, the interview interactions reflect difficulties only for ER. Note the comment above that EE appeared at ease and did cooperate.

Step 4. Continue analysis of selected interactions. Examples given below illustrate some of the typical facets of the logical and relational processes.

Category	Input number	Speaker	Input	Commentary on critical interactions
PROBE (DESC) Q	5	ER:	What kind of work is it?	*Logical issue.* ER succeeded in asking a broader Q, and

Category	Input number	Speaker	Input	Commentary on critical interactions
				asked it on a prior cue from EE. EE gave a relevant response.
FACT	6	EE:	Well, it's in an onion shed. I'm foreman of a crew in charge of loading trucks and boxcars.	*Relational issue.* ER recovered some confidence in his ability to word questions, and has seen that EE is willing to cooperate. EE cooperated, and gave a longer answer.

Explanation. Input 5 was selected because it shows the first sign of improvement in ER's wording of questions. A broader question was called for, and ER did ask one. ER could have recovered more fully in this manner: "I started with too limited a question. Backing off some, I'd like you to tell me about your present work: your responsibilities, the working conditions, your relationships with your superiors and subordinates, and what you like and dislike about the work." Important in this example is the indication that ER is recovering from his initial blunders and is overcoming his initial feelings of mistrust and confusion over the inclusion and control issues.

Category	Input number	Speaker	Input	Commentary on critical interactions
DESC Q	17	ER:	What other kinds of work have you done?	*Logical issue.* ER changed the subject too soon. In input 16, EE has exposed
DESC (FACT)	18	EE:	Oh, I've. . . . I started out driv-	a personal OPIN about the other

ing tractor, and then I worked in a lumber mill driving a fork lift, and . . .

people at work, which should be followed up as an indirect cue about his FEEL about himself. Change is too soon, also, because inadequate d a t a have been obtained about his present work situation.

Relational issue. ER felt dislike for EE, saw EE projecting his irresponsibility onto characteristics of other people. Having jumped to this conclusion, ER inadvertently went on to another topic without trying to get confirmation of it because he disliked EE. ER was influenced more by his feeling of dislike for EE than by cues from EE.

Explanation. This is a common example of one type of logical discontinuity: a change in topic. Such abrupt changes in topic are easily identified after they occur, but tend to come as a surprise to ER when ER does it! Note, in this case, the relational issue was ER's dislike for EE.

Step 5. The last step is to see how the interview ended.

Category	Input number	Speaker	Input	Commentary on critical interactions
OPIN, FEEL	146	EE:	(*EE has expressed several strong opinions and feelings about suicide.*) And I'm just flat a coward. I think about suicide and I'm afraid to pull the trigger.	*Logical issue.* ER cut off the interview very abruptly, after EE expressed strong personal feelings. Logically, ER should have gradually helped EE shift to a less personal level of communication before ending.
RAP	147	ER:	Thanks a lot, Jim. That's the end.	*Relational issue.* ER has empathized with EE, but also is tired of listening to him. The mixed feelings made ER awkward in how to pull away. EE has been controlling the interview, with rambling, circumlocutory statements which took ER back and forth from disgust to empathy. EE appeared very involved, and seemed to enjoy the chance to express himself in such de-

> tail and in the ways
> he chose, uncon-
> trolled by ER.

Explanation. Such an abrupt ending is poor. Ethically, ER should never leave EE "dangling" in the middle of a personal exposure of his feelings. Even the beginning ER can immediately recoup. If he does prematurely end an interview in this way, hopefully he will recognize what he has done and take enough additional time to enable EE to calm down or regain his normal emotional balance.

Other examples of important skills and mistakes in interviewing are given on pp. 147–152.

<table>
<tr><td>

9

</td><td>

HOW TO EVALUATE YOUR INTERVIEWING SKILLS

</td></tr>
</table>

Now it is time to pull all the threads of your interview analysis together. How can you get an overview of your strengths and weaknesses? What can you say about the more objective features of your interview? How can you relate communication theory (Chapter 1) to what you have done? Does your performance satisfy the criteria for skilled ERs?

This is a two-part evaluation. First, you ferret out the impact of extrinsic factors—agency regulations, physical setting, and specific ER and EE roles. Then, you can evaluate the actual interview behaviors—the incidence of different types of inputs, the logical and relational processes, and ER strengths and weaknesses. (See Sections V and VI in the Appendix for more detailed examples of evaluation.)

EVALUATION OF EFFECTS OF EXTRINSIC INFLUENCES

Any interview is affected by factors over which ER and EE have only partial or sometimes no control. Before zeroing in on your ER skills, you may find you are less anxious if you first determine the impact of the extrinsic influences. Analysis of the effects of extrinsic influences made in the Jim Smith interview and explanations of how to do each are given below.

A. AGENCY LIMITATIONS

As a student at a university, ER was expected to comply with general university regulations and with the expectations of the instructor of the course. In this interview, there did not appear to be any organizational limitations that were conflictual with the intended purposes of the practice interview. EE was cooperative when he learned ER was a student at a university.

> **Agency or organizational limitations include any formal or informal policies, regulations, or common practices that relate to the process of interviewing. In this case, constriction was minimal, except in terms of the responsibility of the student to the instructor—rules that show up under the next category of role. In some institutions, specific legal or policy guidelines may mitigate against the accomplishment of the intrinsic purposes of the interview. For example, a simple factor such as amount of time available to do an interview definitely sets the outer limits for what can be done. If an employment interviewer must see thirty people in a day, he cannot spend over fifteen minutes per interview.**

B. ER AND EE ROLES

ER is in a subordinate position as a student. He was expected to conform to several rules laid out by the instructor, including ethical rights of EE, to not attempt to deliberately alter EE's behavior or feelings, and to submit a detailed self-critique of the interview. As part of the requirements for a graded course in interviewing, ER was subject to a dual judgment process: that of the instructor, as well as his own ideas of what interviewing is and how it should be evaluated.

> **First, indicate any specific role expectations related to interviewing. In this instance, the specific rules specified by the instructor are given. If an employee, indicate the guidelines—written or implicit—for the conduct of the interview. Also include whatever evaluation by others**

may be done, and the type of data used to make the evaluation.

ER is relatively inexperienced in the world of work. Hence the subject matter of the interview was fairly novel, making it more difficult to anticipate how to proceed. Further, ER had never had prior experience with the type of EE he had, namely, a person with a history of poor work habits and alleged minor criminal behaviors.

prev. unknown unusual

> **Second, observe ER's exposure to the subject matter and the types of people to be interviewed. If entirely novel to you, you might have more difficulty with the logical processes in the interview.**

EE is a volunteer, which gave him much latitude in how much he chose to cooperate. EE appeared to find the interview situation fairly comfortable and did try to cooperate (but ER's lack of skill, coupled with EE's personality, resulted in a relatively poor interview).

voluntary

> **Third, note the volitional status of EE. In the Jim Smith interview, EE's volunteer status gave him more power to choose how much he would cooperate.**
>
> **A client who enters counseling is electing to submit himself to the influence of the counselor—but for only the particular problems of concern to the client.**
>
> **From his own point of view, a person on unemployment compensation sees the employment counselor (a) to comply with the organizational regulations so he can continue to receive unemployment compensation checks, and/or (b) to genuinely seek help to find work.**
>
> **Last, comment on the degree to which ER and EE roles helped and hindered the actual interview process.**

C. THE PHYSICAL SETTING

The interview was conducted in a closed lounge in ER's dormitory. The setting was comfortable (soft chairs) and quiet. No unexpected interruptions occurred. ER and EE were sitting in soft chairs, with the audio tape recorder on a nearby coffee table. ER and EE were sitting directly opposite each other, about five feet apart, with a coffee table beside the two chairs.

> **Describe the setting. Where was the interview room located? What kind of a room was it? How was the room furnished? Where did ER and EE sit? How far apart? Was any object between them? Where was the recorder? Was there another person in the room to operate the equipment? Were there any interruptions? If so, what was their effect?**

EE seemed ill at ease in the university setting. Before going to the interview room, he asked many questions about what goes on in a college and glanced uneasily around the campus and the dormitory.

> **Describe EE's behavior before entering the interview room.**

At the beginning of the interview, ER was very uneasy. While he had set everything (room, recorder) up in advance so that he would not keep EE waiting, his mind drew a "blank" as he was preparing to begin the interview. ER also felt awkward when turning on the recorder. EE began to appear more at ease once seated in the interview room. EE did watch ER turn on the recorder, but it did not appear to bother him.

> **Describe ER's feelings and behavior at the beginning of the interview. Describe EE's behavior and apparent feelings at the beginning.**

Although EE appeared a bit uneasy at first, ER took longer to become at ease than did EE. There appeared to be no lasting negative effects of the setting on either person. The comfortable chairs and the quiet room seemed to help.

> **Sum up the effects of the setting on ER and EE.**

So much for the extrinsic factors. Now for the second part of the evaluation, the patterns of behavior of ER and EE in the interview.

EVALUATION OF INTERVIEW BEHAVIORS

Now you are ready for a final series of analyses intended to provide an overview of the entire interview. The overview is based on a tabulation of the objective features of the interview (see Figure 3), a summary analysis of the logical and relational processes, and finally a summary of your strengths and weaknesses. The categories of questions and statements ER and EE used in the Jim Smith interview are given in Figure 3; the following is a step-by-step explanation of how to do the tabulation.

A. THE OBJECTIVE COUNT

Step 1. Set up a tabulation sheet similar to Figure 3. Under EE Statements, omit the asterisked items—Mixed FACT, Mixed OPIN, and Mixed FEEL—for the initial tabulation.

Step 2. Begin with input 1. Tally ER's first statement or question. In the Jim Smith interview, input 1 was ER's PUR, so it is tallied under ER Statements.

Step 3. Talley a DBL BAR Q three times—once for each of the two questions, then a third tally for DBL BAR Q. For example, in the Jim Smith interview, ER's third input is DBL BAR Q, including a FACT Q and a LEAD (I) Q. One tally is given in the ER column for each of those three items.

Figure 3. Tabulation of the Objective Features in the Jim Smith Interview

ER Questions			EE Statements		
Category	Number	Percent	Category	Number	Percent
FACT Q	9		FACT	11	
PROBE (FACT) Q	4		DESC (FACT)	0	
DESC Q	1		*Mixed FACT	19	
PROBE (DESC) Q	1		Total FACT	30	43
Total FACT	15	21	OPIN	32	

Figure 3 (continued)

ER Questions

Category	Number	Percent
OPIN Q	14	
PROBE (OPIN) Q	14	
LEAD (U) Q	7	
LEAD (I) Q	10	
PROJ Q	1	
Total OPIN	46	66
FEEL Q	1	
PROBE (FEEL) Q	2	
Total FEEL	3	4
CR EX Q	1	
CF Q	5	
Total	6	8
Total ER Questions	70	100
DBL BAR Q	11	

ER Statements

	Number	Percent
PUR	1	
RAP	2	
ECHO	1	
ENC	8	
NV	0	
GUG	2	
I	3	
AS	6	
ADV	1	
FACT	1	
Total ER Statements	25	

EE Statements

Category	Number	Percent
DESC (OPIN)	3	
*Mixed OPIN	21	
Total OPIN	56	81
FEEL	0	
*Mixed FEEL	8	
Total FEEL	8	12
1. DESC (FACT + OPIN + FEEL)	2	
2. DESC (FACT + OPIN)	10	
3. DESC (FACT + FEEL)	2	
4. DESC (OPIN + FEEL)	0	
5. OPIN + FEEL	4	
6. FACT + OPIN	5	
Total Mixed Statements	23	33
Total EE Statements	69	100

Other Behavior

	Number	Percent
CFS	2	
S	1	
ENC	1	
NV	7	
I	3	
AGR	3	
Total Other Behavior	16	

Step 4. Tally other multiply scored inputs as you did above. For example, in the Jim Smith interview, EE's eighth input is tallied three times—OPIN, NV, and FACT.

Step 5. Under EE Statements, add up EE's Mixed FACT by summing up all the Mixed Categories with FACT in them—numbers 1, 2, 3, and 6. This gives the Mixed FACT total of 19. Make the same calculation for Mixed OPIN (numbers 1, 2, 5, 6) and Mixed FEEL (numbers 1, 3, 5).

Step 6. Add up total number of ER questions, omitting the DBL BAR Q tally. Add up total number of ER statements,

Step 7. Add up total number of EE FACT, OPIN, FEEL, and Mixed Statements, omitting the Mixed FACT, Mixed OPIN, and Mixed FEEL entries. Add up the other EE behaviors.

Step 8. Figure the percent of ER FACT Qs by dividing Total ER FACT Qs (15) *by* Total Qs (70) and enter the quotient (21 percent) in the percentage column. Make similar calculations for ER's OPIN, FEEL, and other questions.

Step 9. Figure the percent of EE Statements by dividing EE total FACT (30) by total FACT, OPIN, FEEL, and Mixed Statements (69) and enter the percentage (43 percent) in the percentage column. Make similar calculations for EE's OPIN, FEEL, and Mixed Statements. Note that the sum of the percentages will add up to well over 100 percent because the Mixed FACT, Mixed OPIN, and Mixed FEEL are duplicate tallies of the entries in Mixed Categories.

B. THE LOGICAL PROCESS

What was ER's skill in the use of the logical process? What was the impact of EE's style of logical communication on ER? Using the results of the analyses of the manifest content, the categorization of inputs, the objective count, and the analysis of critical interactions, here are some conclusions.

> **Arrange these materials for easy viewing: the manifest content analysis, the transcript with inputs categorized, the analysis of critical interactions, and the objective count. Proceed to the next step.**

1. *Ratios of* FACT, OPIN, FEEL *inputs.* The plan for this interview called for about an equal ratio of OPIN and FEEL interactions, with about 20 percent FACT to define the specifics of each topic. ER asked 15 FACT Qs, 46 OPIN Qs, and 3 FEEL Qs: 21 percent, 66 percent, and 4 percent, respectively. The FACT percentage is close to that expected. The OPIN Qs were excessively high, with far too few FEEL Qs. FEEL information often was implied in the OPIN Qs, especially the LEAD Qs, but ER failed to probe enough to elicit specific FEEL statements from EE.

Review your interview plan and estimate what the "ideal" ratio might be. All interviews need a factual base. A good ratio in a depth interview is between 15 percent and 25 percent. In a depth interview which surveys a major area of the EE's thinking and feeling, a good ratio would be half OPIN and half FEEL. (In the Jim Smith interview, it was 40 percent each.)

If fewer than 15 percent FACT Qs were asked, the interview may suffer from a lack of an adequate foundation of factual information. A symptom of such a lack is redundancy—repeating a topic several times. Another symptom is lack of EE cooperation on OPIN and FEEL questions or excessive EE defensiveness or rationalization, resulting in refusal of EE to expose his inner reactions.

If the interview ran much higher than 25 percent FACT Qs, it indicates ER was too anxious to be able to ask for more personal OPIN and/or FEEL information from EE. Evidence for this tendency showed up in the analysis of critical interactions, in which ER was found to move away from EE's more personal cues and ask impersonal FACT Qs.

Inexperienced interviewers tend to excel at asking OPIN Qs and are least skillful in asking FEEL Qs. The Jim Smith interview is typical: there, ER was facile in formulating OPIN Qs 66 percent of the time, but inept in wording FEEL Qs—**he was facile only 4 percent of the time.**

EE's ratios were 30 FACT, 56 OPIN, and 8 FEEL—43 percent, 81 percent, and 12 percent, respectively. Thus, EE communicated almost exclusively at the levels of FACT and OPIN, consonant with ER's pattern. With 33 percent of EE's inputs being mixed, however, EE was constantly shifting logical levels, which makes it difficult to infer what EE's real opinions and feelings were.

> **Next, examine EE's ratios. Look for EE's dominant mode of expression and for the impact of his ratio of mixed inputs. In the Jim Smith interview, EE is highly oriented to OPIN, with 81 percent, and more moderately oriented to FACT, with 43 percent; FEEL runs a very low third place. This pattern indicates a strong logical orientation toward abstraction, with facts interspersed to support the abstractions, but with little real exposure of EE's inner reactions or details of his life.**

Compared to ER's ratios, EE emitted twice as many FACT inputs, a few more OPIN inputs, and twice as many FEEL inputs. This differential ratio, combined with EE's high percentage of mixed inputs, indicates a rather jerky, discontinuous interview.

> **Last, compare EE's ratios to ER's. If they match across FACT, OPIN, and FEEL, is that evidence of a relatively smooth, continuous flow across logical levels? Check the critical interactions for supporting evidence. If the ratios are more than 10 percent different, this is evidence of discontinuity in the logical levels. A high rate of mixed inputs often accounts for such a discrepancy, as it does in the Jim Smith interview. What is the criterion for mixed EE inputs in a good interview? With good logical interactions, ER should be able to get EE to limit mixed inputs after the first ten or fifteen minutes, so that 10 percent of EE's inputs might be mixed. Note the 33 per-**

cent mixed inputs in the Jim Smith interview, three times as high as the ideal percentage. This criterion does not apply, of course, to an EE who is acutely disturbed.

2. *Probing and the use of EE cues.* ER asked 21 PROBE QS out of a total of 70. A more skillful ER would have asked five to ten more PROBE QS. Most (24) of the probing was in the OPIN category, indicating that ER was more likely to try to focus on EE's opinions than EE's facts or feelings.

> How much did ER use the cues EE gave? To probe is to pick up on data EE has given and to continue to pursue a topic by narrowing it down to specifics. Thus, the skillful ER is constantly matching up his prior questions with leads given by EE and formulating a PROBE Q which gets closer to a target. Hence the skilled ER asks at least 50 percent PROBE QS.
>
> Count these question categories as PROBE QS: PROBE (FACT) Q, PROBE (DESC) Q, PROBE (OPIN) Q, LEAD (I) Q, and PROBE (FEEL) Q.

From the critique of the critical interactions, ER failed to probe because he changed the topic abruptly five times (ER inputs 11, 17, 25, 51, 147) and shifted the level of communication too quickly ten times (ER inputs 3, 9, 21, 29, 59, 73, 81, 105, 131, 141).

> Examine the critical interactions for the incidence of logical discontinuity. Note both ER's premature shifts in topic and his too abrupt shifts in level of communication.

ER did show some ability to follow through on EE cues, by staying on the same topic and probing well (ER inputs 11, 15, 27, 41, 55, 89, 121).

> Examine the critical interactions for examples of good probing.

3. *ER's ability to word and focus questions.* After some initial

stumbling in the wording of questions, ER did well in the clarity of the questions he asked. While there were too many DBL BAR Qs, the eleven incidents were not severely damaging to EE's responses. Clarity is indicated by the occurrence of only two EE CFSs and no EE CFQs. The one ER ECHO is also a positive indicator of good ER control of his verbalizations.

> **Examine DBL BAR Qs—their frequency and effects on EE responses. A good ER asks no DBL BAR Qs. Another source of evidence is EE's CFSs and CFQs. Here, the criterion is none or very few. ER's ECHOs are a third source of data. If really caught off guard by an EE answer, ER will tend to mimic or repeat the answer. Here, too, the criterion is none or very few.**

This EE was fairly cooperative and often gave informative responses even though ER tended to ask too many closed-ended questions.

> **Next, examine ER's ability to shift the breadth of focus in his questions. If EE has been cooperative and informative on a prior question, ER may show confidence in EE's cooperation by asking broader questions. If EE has been uncooperative or difficult to pin down on a question (usually a FEEL Q or a very specific OPIN Q), ER may show EE his lack of cooperation by using a narrowly focused question. This section evaluates ER's ability to alter the breadth of his questions, depending on what kinds of responses he has been getting from the EE.**

At the beginning of the interview, ER used narrowly focused FACT and OPIN Qs when these were not indicated. The first LEAD (I) Q, input 3, was premature. The second LEAD (I) Q, input 81, was not skillful in that it narrowed the communication too fast. The next two OPIN Qs, 89 and 91, were good attemps to draw out the more specific feeling tones of EE's previous inputs. The next two LEAD (I) Qs, inputs 99 and 103, were unskillful because they were almost like advice-giving. The LEAD (I) Q in input 131 again narrowed the communication too fast; ER should have used a broader PROBE (OPIN) Q first. The last LEAD (I) Q in input 135 is again more like advice-giving.

> Skillful interviewers use LEAD (I) Qs only when EE is too vague. Most often, LEAD (I) Qs are used to pin down a particular feeling EE has partially exposed. Before using a very narrow question, ER should have gradually narrowed the focus by first using a broad DESC or OPIN Q or an open-ended FEEL Q (i.e., "How did that make you feel?"), then a narrower PROBE Q. If EE still is vague, then a LEAD (I) Q may be tried. If successful, EE then usually exposes quite a bit more information. If unsuccessful, EE may just say "yes" or "no," leaving it up to ER to guess whether the assumption in his LEAD (I) Q was correct!

ER asked seven unskillful LEAD (U) Qs.

> No LEAD (U) Qs should be asked.

ER used one PROJ Q and no SUP Qs. ER was too busy trying to sort out the direct control of the interactions and did not think of using indirect methods. The one PROJ Q was effective.

> Last, examine ER's use of indirect questions, such as the SUP Q and the PROJ Q. Skillful ERs use the indirect question when EE has had considerable difficulty answering direct OPIN or FEEL Qs. By shifting the object to a future or imaginal fantasy (SUP Q) or to the EE's notions of what someone else is like (PROJ Q), EE may find it easier to expose himself. Inexperienced ERs may use the SUP Q as a variant of advice-giving ("If you don't find a better job, what do you think will happen to you and your family?").
>
> A successful indirect question usually has to be followed by more direct questions to give an accurate picture of EE's own OPINS and FEELS.

4. *Conclusions from manifest content analysis.* In the original plan, there were 19 subtopics; four new subtopics were added during the interview. ER covered eight of the original 19 subtopics with some degree of adequacy; none of the new subtopics was fully explored. This performance falls well below an 80 percent criterion. EE was preoccupied with ruminations about his negative self-image, so ER was successful on those subtopics relating to EE's self-image. When ER tried to lead EE into other topics, EE tended to reiterate his common theme of depression and failure. Since ER used very few FEEL Qs, EE may have been induced by ER's failure to validate his feelings to continuously repeat himself.

> **Count up the number of subtopics on the original plan, plus the number of new subtopics added. The criterion is 80 to 90 percent coverage of old and new subtopics.**
>
> **Identify what kept ER from covering more of the intended content.**

C. THE RELATIONAL PROCESS

What was ER's skill in the relational processes? What was the impact of EE's verbal and nonverbal styles of relational communication on ER? Conclusions are drawn from the the data in the objective count, the categorization of inputs, the critique of critical interactions, and the above analysis of the logical process.

> **Use the same materials as you did above for the logical process analysis. You may not need the manifest content analysis.**

1. *ER's feedback to EE.* ER used no SUM or REFL to give feedback to EE.

ER used one CR EX Q in input 53; it was skillfully done to check about EE's owing back rent.

ER used two RAP statements at the end of the interview. He could have used several more. Those used at the end were not effective because the ending was too abrupt. ER did use eight verbalized ENCs, improving in the second half of the interview.

The eight ENCs average about one per every nine EE inputs, not quite frequent enough to give EE adequate verbal feedback. Eye contact was more frequent in the second half.

> **How often, and how clearly, did ER give feedback to EE? Better interviewers use SUM, REFL, reiteration of a FACT, and sometimes CR EX Q to give feedback to EE about what he has been saying—both to show ER has been listening, and to encourage EE to expose himself more. ENC and RAP also may be used.**
>
> **A good interview has several SUMS and REFLS, and reiteration of a FACT or CR EX Q is used only when EE appears to be contradicting himself and is elusive about the contradiction. SUM is used with FACTS and OPINS, while REFL is used with FEELS.**
>
> **For ENC, the criterion is a moderate number, roughly one for every five to eight EE inputs. A lower number indicates inadequate verbal feedback to EE that ER is listening. A higher number indicates ER is tending toward interrupting or overcontrolling.**
>
> **Cite trends in eye contact.**

While ER repeatedly was frustrated with EE's defensiveness and pessimistic self-ruminations, ER did not show a skill in explicitly giving EE feedback about their relationship.

> **If repeatedly faced with lack of cooperation from EE, a skilled ER may explicitly raise the issue of the relational process between ER and EE. You may want to review Chapter 1 for the earmarks of effective relational communication.**

ER made six AS and one ADV statements. As seen in the analysis of critical interactions, ER had a difficult time converting his dislike for EE into a facilitative channel for communication with EE. The AS and ADV verbally show ER's opinions about what EE is like and what EE should do. This was a major weakness throughout the interview.

There should be no AS, ADV, AGR, or DISAGR on the part of ER in an information-gathering interview. All of these categories indicate ER was unable to channel his personal reactions and opinions in a facilitative way with EE. Rather, their occurrence shows that ER impulsively stated his opinions about what EE is like or what EE should do. AGR or DISAGR by ER show he has been caught off guard and feels compelled to show his support or lack of support for an assertion by EE. All four types of ER input tend to cut off further EE response or make EE defensive.

2. *Control of the interview by the pacing.*

Some of the control process shows in the pacing of the interview. Pacing may be assessed in several ways.

The 147 inputs divided by 65 minutes of interview time yield a per-minute input rate of about 2.3, which is within the desirable range. Hence, the rate of interaction and length of EE inputs were adequate in this interview.

First, calculate a per-minute rate of inputs by dividing the total number of ER and EE inputs by the length of the interview in minutes. The rate per minute for a 60-minute depth interview should be between two and four inputs per minute. A higher rate indicates ER failed to get EE to make statements of adequate length to get relevant facts and opinions. A lower rate indicates that EE talked too long per EE input, making it difficult for ER to control the topics being discussed and/or the appropriate level of communication needed.

ER used no CS or PS. This indicates ER was posing his next questions too fast. ER needs to develop a slower pacing by using CS.

Second, evaluate the pauses. A skilled ER frequently uses the courtesy pause—at least once every five minutes —to allow EE to reflect on what he has just said.

ER had no ANTs, two GUGs, and three Is. EE had three Is. While low in number, the eight disruptive behaviors reflect uneven pacing.

> **Third, evaluate the frequency of ANT, GUG, and I. Except for overtalkative EEs, the experienced ER seldom ANTS, GUGS, or IS. The more uneven the level of communication between ER and EE, the more GUGS and IS appear.**

Overall, the pace appeared adequate, but can be improved by using CS and reducing interruptive inputs.

> **Sum up the data on pace of the interview.**

3. *ER and EE styles of* NV *communication.* EE's main NV vocal behavior was a nervous laughter, which stopped about halfway through the interview. This indicates ER was helping EE to be somewhat more comfortable. Initially, this EE NV behavior was disruptive to ER. EE's other vocal features were difficult to read. He tended to have the same inflections and tonal qualities at all levels of expression.

EE's eye contact with ER was poor at the beginning, but soon improved as he seemed to get comfortable in the interview room. EE conveyed an interest in following ER's lead with the eye contact.

Both EE and ER were relatively immobile, in terms of body position, arm and hand gestures, and unrelated body movements. The stillness of these movements perhaps reflected a moderate level of tension which lasted throughout the interview.

EE's facial expressions were largely indirect. He sometimes smiled when he was expressing negative feelings about himself— almost pleading with ER to support him. He sometimes frowned when he talked about his goals, conveying a desire not to talk about the positives in his life.

> **Much of the emotional impact of interpersonal interactions is in the myriad of behaviors that accompany the verbal expressions of ER and EE. The nonverbal**

realm includes auditory cues such as sighing, laughter, crying, coughing, as well as vocal overtones (loud–quiet, tense–smooth, close–distant); visual cues such as facial expressions, hand gestures, body position, leg movements; body movements apparently unrelated to the meaning of a message, such as an EE pulling his ear lobe or putting his hand over his eyes. (These and other cues, such as eye contact, were reviewed in Chapter 3.) The criterion is the directness of the nonverbal expressions. That is, were ER's nonverbal expressions consonant with his verbalizations? How much did EE throw ER off track by indirect nonverbal expressions?

ER did not show tension by vocal NV expressions. While ER's voice initially was tense, higher pitched than normal, his voice became lower pitched, warmer, with well-modulated volume as the interview went on. ER has good voice quality, although this asset was not sufficient to compensate for some of the major lacks of skill noted in earlier parts of the analysis.

Include data on ER's vocal qualities, whether using audio or video equipment.

ER used numerous facial expressions to give EE additional feedback about his reactions to EE. ER used good eye contact throughout the interview. ER showed interest and empathy much of the time. But ER also showed dislike and disdain in his facial expressions when he was most affected by his dislike for EE. All of these facial expressions tended, however, to be direct rather than indirect.

When using video playback, you may also observe the many other nonverbal dimensions of ER's behavior.

4. *Summary: inclusion felt by ER and EE.* ER experienced a strong feeling of commitment initially, but was frequently discouraged by EE's answers, which ER construed as uninformative. Hence, ER waivered between high inclusion and moderate inclusion.

EE often appeared to feel included, because many of his responses were actually what ER asked for. EE's indirect non-verbal communications were distracting and conveyed an avoidance of involvement. Since ER was rather unskillful in drawing EE out, EE may have felt only halfway committed to the interview. EE was willing to expose himself up to a point—to the degree he apparently had already thought through his situation and problems—but was unwilling to think and feel more deeply. This conclusion must be tempered, however, by ER's lack of control of the interview.

> **Sum up the evidences for the degree to which ER and EE felt "in" or "out" of the interview process.**

5. *Summary: control processes.* ER lost control of the interview many times, by starting off incorrectly and by allowing EE to repeat himself and communicate at mixed levels. ER also evaded deeper personal expressions by EE, often failing to probe on FEEL cues EE gave.

EE appeared to feel inferior to ER, especially when he first arrived on campus. EE's verbal behavior was largely controlling, however, since it is doubtful if EE revealed anything he had not previously anticipated.

> **Sum up the evidences for the degree to which ER and EE felt "on top" or "on bottom" in the process of the control of the interactions.**

6. *Summary: affection felt by ER and EE.* EE gave ER very few cues about how much he liked or disliked ER. At times, EE appeared to be spontaneously enjoying the communication, but he also quickly retreated and became more distant.

ER switched back and forth from a strong dislike of EE and his apparent lack of responsibility, to a feeling of empathy—more like sorrow—for EE.

> **Sum up the evidence for the degree to which ER and EE liked or disliked each other.**

D. BALANCE BETWEEN LOGICAL AND RELATIONAL PROCESSES

What was ER's skill in balancing the logical and relational processes? How well did EE balance the logical and relational issues, and what was the impact of EE's style on ER? How much did ER do to guide EE into a logical and relational balance that would accomplish the purposes of the interview?

In the last two sections we considered the logical and relational processes separately. This section puts the two processes together, as they actually do go together in any behavior. A key criterion is balance: if the communication is logically poor, what did ER do to correct it? If the communication was overloaded relationally or emotionally, what was the effect on ER, and what did he do logically or relationally to recover the appropriate direction of interaction?

1. *EE's logical and relational styles of communicating.* EE was highly preoccupied with an intermingled set of facts, opinions, and feelings centered around a very poor image of himself. EE refused to explore other topics in any depth, especially in relation to his interactions with significant other people in his environment. EE's strong preoccupation with a limited area of his experience made him very inflexible, both logically and relationally. EE seemed almost unaware of his own patterns of verbal and nonverbal communication. Yet his impact on ER dominated the interactions.

Sum up the characteristics of EE's verbal and nonverbal behaviors. Assess the evidence for EE's self-awareness of his logical and relational styles.

2. *ER's logical and relational styles of communicating.* ER did show a wide range of verbal and nonverbal behaviors throughout the interview, both skillful and unskillful. ER was strongly affected by two negative feelings: fear of EE's lack of commitment to the interview and dislike of EE's lack of responsibility. While ER did overcome these feelings several times during the inter-

view and made some logical progress, he let them regain control and could not constructively channel them into the logical and relational issues as they occurred in the interactions.

Sum up the characteristics of ER's verbal and nonverbal behaviors. Assess the evidence of ER's self-awareness and ability to cope with his logical and relational experiences.

E. SUMMARY OF ER STRENGTHS AND WEAKNESSES

Make a list of the ER strengths and weaknesses you have noted in all of the analyses in Chapters 6–8. Cite the portion of the analysis from which the items came. The references in parentheses in our list here are to the appropriate portions of the analysis of the Jim Smith interview in the Appendix. The purpose of the list is to serve as a brief reminder to you. You may use it to compare with a second analysis, if you do another one. With two or more analyses, you may compare how you react to different interview settings, different EEs, and different interview purposes.

ER strengths

1. ER held to the main outline of the planned topics (III.A). ER did especially well in covering EE's personal adjustment and reactions to his problems (III.A and B).
2. ER asked an adequate percentage of FACT Qs (VI.B.1).
3. ER did explain PUR (IV).
4. ER used PROJ Q well (IV).
5. ER probed for OPIN (VI.B.2).
6. ER worded questions well (VI.B.3).
7. ER's overall pacing was adequate (VI.C.2).
8. ER had good voice quality (VI.C.3).
9. ER offered direct, communicative nonverbal expressions to EE (VI.C.3).

ER weaknesses

1. ER failed to cover adequately EE's interpersonal experiences. When ER added new topics, he failed to get enough data (III.A and B).

2. ER omitted a review of the ethics and the TOPIC (IV).
3. ER asked too many OPIN Qs and too few FEEL Qs (VI.B.1).
4. ER failed to disentangle EE's FEEL inputs from EE's many mixed inputs (VI.B.1).
5. ER did poorly in handling the flow of logical issues in the interview, failing to probe many times, and changing the topic too abruptly five times (VI.B.2).
6. ER needs more practice in use of indirect questions (VI.B.3).
7. ER used too many LEAD (U) Qs (VI.B.4).
8. ER needs extensive practice in giving feedback to EE, especially use of SUM, REFL, ENC, and RAP (VI.C.1).
9. ER used too much AS and ADV, reflecting his relational problems with EE (VI.C.1).
10. ER made questions too narrow, before asking broader questions (VI.B.3).
11. ER used LEAD (I) Q prematurely and implied he was giving advice (VI.B.3).
12. ER needs more practice in the use of CS and reduction of GUGs and IS (VI.C.2).
13. ER lost control of the interview many times (VI.C.5).
14. ER was sometimes incapacitated by a strong dislike of EE (VI.C.6).

You have completed the detailed critique of your interview. Students find the first time through the analysis pretty difficult—and painful! It is not easy to reflect on and dissect one's behavior! You now have some idea of a theory of interpersonal relations, which will help you understand the interviewing process. You have learned about the especially difficult matter of experiencing the feelings involved in relational issues. You know how to plan and conduct a practice interview. You have done a content analysis of the manifest content of your interview, to see how adequate your coverage was. You have learned how to categorize ER and EE inputs in order to analyze the patterns of logical and relational interactions. You have applied the interpersonal theory to a selected few critical interview interactions to see what was happening to you and the EE.

The list of your strengths and weaknesses as an interviewer poses a challenge: How do you get practice to reinforce your strengths and to correct your weaknesses? Can you further compensate for some of the weaknesses by using your strengths more? And, the question we began with in the Preface: "Can you make your next interview better?" I hope your answer is a loud, confident "Yes!"

APPENDIX
THE JIM SMITH INTERVIEW:
An Example of a Complete Write-up of an Interview

OUTLINE OF THE INTERVIEW WRITE-UP

I. The interview plan
  A. The role relationships of ER and EE
  B. Formulation of the problem
  C. Outputs
  D. EE inputs

II. The Interview transcript

III. Manifest content analysis
  A. EE inputs
  B. Outputs

IV. Commentary on critical interactions

V. Effects of extrinsic influences
  A. Agency limitations
  B. ER and EE roles
  C. The physical setting

VI. Evaluation of interview behaviors
  A. The objective count
  B. The logical process
  C. The relational process
  D. Balance between logical and relational processes
  E. Summary of ER strengths and weaknesses

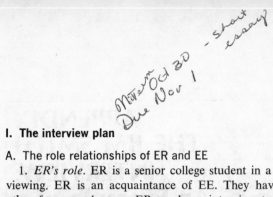

I. The interview plan

A. The role relationships of ER and EE

1. *ER's role.* ER is a senior college student in a course on interviewing. ER is an acquaintance of EE. They have not seen each other for several years. ER needs an interview to practice for his interviewing course. ER is expecting EE to cooperate in the interview in order to give ER interview experience. ER thinks EE is facing a situation which EE needs to resolve.

2. *EE's role.* EE is a 20-year-old male, high-school dropout, working as a day laborer. ER has contacted EE by phone and explained briefly the purpose of the interview. EE stated he is willing to start the interview but is unsure how fully he will want to cooperate. No specifics of the interview plan were discussed.

B. Formulation of the problem — *any terms of EE*

1. *Description of the problem.* From past knowledge, ER believes EE has persistently failed to accomplish meaningful goals academically and vocationally. ER is interested in helping EE analyze the forces which maintain EE in his present pattern of behavior and evaluating what EE may wish to do to change the situation.

Guess — Vague idea of something. Wrong.

2. *Information available.* EE has held and been fired from (or quit) six manual labor jobs in the last six months. From contacts with relatives, ER believes EE still owes money to numerous friends, relatives, and creditors. It is rumored by his relatives that he has written several bad checks. He has had several minor run-ins with the law but has never been arrested.

C. Outputs *As a result of the interview, I will find out*

The report. Since this is a voluntary interview intended to give ER practice, the report is to be directed to the instructor who will be the only person to read it. It will not be shown to EE.

1. *A description of Jim's self-concept.* How he perceives his present pattern of behavior; what his goals are; what he thinks prevents/helps him reach his goals.

2. *A prognosis of Jim's future behavior.* How likely is he to change? How will he cope with the problems he has not yet resolved?

Should be suggested by content of the interview. (handwritten margin note)

Interview form (handwritten margin note)

D. EE inputs

1. *Jim's description of his present situation*
   a. Work
   b. Finances
   c. Personal adjustments
   d. Social relationships
   e. Relations with relatives

   — demographic info gathered in interview (handwritten)
   Neighborhood — anything having bearing on subject. (handwritten)

2. *Jim's perceptions of the effects of his present situation on himself* *feelings* ① (handwritten)
   a. What satisfactions/dissatisfactions does he now experience?
   b. What does he see as the reasons or causes of the satisfactions/dissatisfactions he now experiences?
   c. How does he react emotionally to his usual pattern of functioning?

3. *Jim's description and explanation of his goals* *facts* ② (handwritten)
   a. What are his immediate goals?
   b. What are his long-term goals?
   c. What does he think helps him reach his goals?
   d. What does he think hinders him in reaching his goals?
   e. How much help/hindrance does he attribute to others?
   f. How much help/hindrance does he attribute to his own efforts?

4. *Jim's evaluation of his potential for reaching his goals* ③ *opinion attitude* (handwritten)
   a. What does he think would have to change in himself?
   b. What does he think would have to change in others?
   c. How likely does he think he is to change himself?
   d. How likely does he think others are to change?

II. The interview transcript

EE: Jim Smith
ER: Don Brown
Date: December 4, 1966

Category	Transcript	Planned input number
PUR	1. ER: Jim, this is just a demonstration interview on my part. I am doing this as an assignment for a class. We're required to interview someone, and it's practice for us in asking questions and analyzing our style.	
AGR	2. EE: Okay.	
FACT Q, LEAD (I) Q, DBL BAR Q	3. ER: a. What are you doing right now? b. Are you working?	
FACT	4. EE: Yeh, I'm working out in Somersville.	1a
PROBE (DESC) Q	5. ER: What kind of work is it?	
FACT	6. EE: Well, it's in an onion shed. I'm foreman of a crew in charge of loading trucks and boxcars.	1a
FACT Q	7. ER: What kind of hours do you work?	
OPIN, NV, FACT	8. EE: a. God-awful hours. b. (*Laughter*) c. I usually work about 10 to 12 hours a day.	2a
PROBE (OPIN) Q	9. ER: Do you like that kind of work?	

OPIN	10. EE:	No.	2a
FACT Q	11. ER:	Have you thought about getting any other kind?	
FACT	12. EE:	Yeah, I will in January.	3a
FACT Q	13. ER:	What do you plan to do?	
FACT	14. EE:	I'm gonna work for Jones' Delivery, driving a delivery truck.	3a
OPIN Q	15. ER:	Why don't you like it?	
OPIN	16. EE:	Oh, I don't care for the people. They're —well, I am too—they're simple. They come to work, and they go home, and they eat and they go to bed, and that's the way their whole life goes. They come to Somersville, and it's like going to New York for them.	2b
DESC Q	17. ER:	What other kinds of work have you done?	
DESC (FACT)	18. EE:	Oh, I've . . . I started out driving tractor, and then I worked in a lumber mill driving a fork lift, and I worked for Hernandez Road Boring, digging tunnels, and working on the boring machine, and let me see—then I worked on a tugboat for a while, and I've done quite a bit of farm labor off and on, between my gainful employment.	New 5a
OPIN Q	19. ER:	Is there any of these that you particularly liked?	
OPIN	20. EE:	I liked working on tugboats pretty well.	New 6a
OPIN Q	21. ER:	Why aren't you still doing that?	
FEEL, NV, DESC (FACT, OPIN)	22. EE:	a. I, ah, a little afraid of falling overboard (*laughs*). b. After the first two trips, the captain, the mate, and the oiler and the port captain and the personnel manager review what you've done and how you	New 6b

work, and they all vote as to whether you're good enough to stay on or not, and you have to have 100 percent on your side or you don't go back, and I made like 99 percent—all but one thought I was good enough.

OPIN Q, DBL BAR Q

23. ER: Do you think—why do you think that one disagreed?

OPIN

24. EE: Oh, I don't know . . . he . . . I . . . I wasn't his type, I guess.

New
6b

OPIN Q, AS

25. ER: a. How come you changed jobs?
b. You've held quite a few jobs.

DESC (FACT, OPIN)

26. EE: Oh! Well, I get fired a lot, and I've had a lot of work that was just seasonal, and I quit work at driving tractor so I could get a better job at the mill, and I didn't like working at the mill at all, so I quit there to work for Hernandez and I got fired there a couple times—four to be exact.

6b

OPIN Q

27. ER: How come you got fired so often?

DESC (FACT, OPIN), NV

28. EE: a. Well, I'd get tired of working after a while and I'd kind of goof off for a while, show up late, and they fired me, and hired me back a month later. I'd be good for a while and they'd fire me. And I'd be out of work for another month or so.
b. Other than that, I'm a pretty good hand (*laughs*).

6b

PROBE (FACT) Q

29. ER: They hired you back a couple times . . .

I, CFS

30. EE: They hired me back four times. They hired me back four times.

5a

OPIN Q   31. ER: Why do you figure they hired you back?

DESC   32. EE: Well, I'm all right as long as I'm work-   6b
(OPIN,   ing (*laughs*). I'm . . . believe me, I'm
FACT)   okay as long as I'm working, I mean,
NV   you know, it's so. And then I start
           goofing off. Actually, a couple, one of
           the times especially, the old man was
           getting a little short and we'd just kind
           of screwed up a tunnel, and I made
           mistakes, but I mean it wasn't anything
           he had to get all bent out of shape
           about. But I got fired that night. The
           only thing I ever heard about it was be-
           cause I threw a pipe clamp on a bag of
           Bentanite mix and I tore the sack and it
           didn't make the old man very happy.
           And I got fired that night.

AS,   33. ER: Well, if you work steady, they keep you
PROBE   on. How come you start to slack off?
(OPIN)
Q

DESC   34. EE: I've never actually worked that steady   New
(FACT,   there. It's always averaged out about   5a
OPIN)   three days a week in the good times,
           and when we get on a job and get good
           hours, I'd work good, and then the job
           would get done, and then I'd be work-
           ing in the yard, which I didn't like any-
           way; that's one place I slacked off quite
           a bit in the yard. I'd always show up
           late, and I'd work two, three days a
           week.

OPIN Q,   35. ER: Are you looking forward to this job in
CFQ,   January? With James?
DBL
BAR Q

CFS	36. EE:	Jones' Delivery.
ECHO	37. ER:	Jones' Delivery.
OPIN	38. EE:	Yeah, I think I'm going to like driving. I've driven truck before, you know, not as a professional and just doing it as part of the job. And I like driving things pretty well.
LEAD (U) Q	39. ER:	Do you see any chance for advancement at Jones'?
DESC (OPIN)	40. EE:	Yeah, according to the guy I was talking to, the guy that is gonna recommend me, there's a . . . the guys working down there are kind of clods, they do exactly what they're supposed to do and nothing else. They don't put out any effort. I guess if you put out a little bit of effort, and do a few extra things around there, you can advance up pretty fast.
PROBE (OPIN) Q	41. ER:	What would you like to do?
S	42. EE:	(*Silence*)
CFQ	43. ER:	What would you like to advance to?
OPIN	44. EE:	Well, I don't know. I mean I don't know what you can advance to.
LEAD (U) Q	45. ER:	Do you still owe money on your car?
FACT	46. EE:	Oh yeah, yeah, yeah.
FACT Q	47. ER:	Do you owe other debts?
DESC (FACT, OPIN), NV	48. EE:	Well, outside of some back rent, no. And well, back rent and a few bad checks (*laughs*). I, ah, I'm not that actually far behind right now. It's just that I can't stop. I mean, it's enough if I stop working and went to school, I'd

The right-margin codes read, top to bottom: 3a (line 38), 3c (line 40), 3a (line 44), 1b (line 46), 1b (line 48), 3d (line 48).

		never make it. I couldn't make enough money to pay for it.
FACT, PROBE (OPIN) Q	49. ER:	You mentioned bad checks. Why did you write bad checks?
DESC (OPIN, FACT)	50. EE:	Ummm . . . I wasn't working then. New There was the fact that even though 6b you're not working, you still gotta eat. And I didn't have any money and I figured it would be a lot better to cash a few bad checks and eat than to be safe and not eat, and so I cashed some bad checks.
FACT Q	51. ER:	Are you living by yourself?
FACT	52. EE:	Yeah. I live by myself in the front seat 1c of my car.
CR EX Q	53. ER:	I thought you said you owed some back rent.
FACT	54. EE:	Yeah, that's why I'm living in the front 1c seat of my car. I got evicted about . . . it's been about two weeks now . . . a little over two weeks.
PROBE (FEEL) Q	55. ER:	How do you feel about that?
FEEL, OPIN	56. EE:	Oh, it kind of irritates me in a way. I 2b gotta blame it on someone other than myself. Who is . . . I mean it's my fault really, I feel that that's kinda a little bit of human nature. I don't want to blame it on myself so I blame it on my landlady, who's a natural scapegoat, and everytime I think about her, I curse a little bit, then go on. I don't worry about things as much as I should. I

mean I worry about things that don't need worrying about, and things that I should worry about, I chuckle a little bit, and curse and pass on and worry about something unimportant.

PROBE
(FACT)
Q
57. ER: What do you worry about?

FACT,
OPIN
58. EE: Oh-h-h, where I'm going to eat next. Things like that. I mean instead of worrying about other people, I worry about myself too much.

OPIN Q,
FACT
Q, DBL
BAR Q
59. ER: Well, how about other people's feelings toward you? Are your parents still living? 2c

FACT
60. EE: My mother is not. My dad is mentally ill, and he doesn't recognize me when he sees me. 1e

OPIN Q
61. ER: How about your brothers and sisters?

OPIN
62. EE: Oh they don't . . . I mean, we fight and argue like ordinary brothers and sisters, a little more so now and then. 1e

LEAD
(U) Q
63. ER: Do you see them often?

FACT,
OPIN
64. EE: Yeah, I see all my brothers, except my brother in Wintersville. It's kind of a long drive, but I get up there as often as I can. I get along with all my brothers. 1e

PROBE
(OPIN)
Q
65. ER: How do they feel about your . . . your . . . ah . . . debts?

OPIN
66. EE: Well . . .

I, OPIN Q
67. ER: Problems with work?

OPIN,
FACT
68. EE: What they don't know won't hurt them. Most of them don't know what 1b

		I'm doing. I don't think any of my brothers know I've been evicted yet. And, actually, everything else I'm caught up on. None of my brothers know I cashed those bad checks.	1e
PROBE (FACT) Q	69. ER:	Have you paid them up?	
FACT, NV	70. EE:	No. They . . . right now, they are just getting around to banging on my landlady's door. They haven't found me again yet (*laughter*).	1b
PROBE (FACT) Q	71. ER:	How much were the checks for?	
FACT	72. EE:	Oh, they averaged four and five and six dollars. I don't know how much they all are together. There's a bunch of them, about 15 of them, I think.	1b
LEAD (U) Q	73. ER:	Do you plan to pay them off?	
OPIN	74. EE:	If I can, yeah. I mean, not in the immediate future, because I'm not making that kind of money right now. I can't even afford to get an apartment right now. I'm just trying to catch up on the things I missed in the month here.	3a
FACT Q, CFQ, DBL BAR Q	75. ER:	Where do you live? You're not living in an apartment right now?	
FACT	76. EE:	No, I'm living in my car.	1c
FACT Q, FACT Q, DBL BAR Q	77. ER:	Do you . . . ah . . . ever go over and stay with your brothers? Have you ever thought of doing that?	

DESC (FACT, OPIN)	78. EE:	Well, I . . . ah . . . stayed with my older brother, well, off and on for about a year, up until, well, I moved out for good oh about eight, nine months ago, and my older brother is actually the only, I mean I'd even think about, because there's room and he doesn't quite have the financial problems my other brothers have, and but just for the fact that I have lived there, it's not, I mean, you don't want to go moving in on your brother and his family just because you are out of luck and it's not his fault, so I leave him well enough alone, well I just leave him alone.	1e
LEAD (U) Q, CFQ, DBL BAR Q	79. ER:	Do you agree with your landlady for kicking you out? Don't you think she could have given you a little credit?	
DESC (FEEL, FACT)	80. EE:	Well, the thing is, that kinda does actually burn me up, is I was two months behind, and there were other times I'd been three, going on four months behind, and she'd say, well, get it in when you can and she'd paid my rent for me and then I'd pay her the money, and she'd always come down, and I'd go. I figured she'd at least leave me a note. I just came home off a date one night and I found a note one night saying I'd been evicted and that was it.	1b
FEEL Q, LEAD (I) Q, DBL BAR Q	81. ER:	How does this affect you? What do you feel, with bad checks, you're liable to have the cops after you after a while, don't you think?	

DESC   82. EE: Oh, yeah, eventually, but like I say, I   1c
(OPIN)   don't worry about the things I should
                 worry about. Well, actually, there is
                 nothing I can do about it now. Because
                 there is nothing I can do about it now,
                 I mean if they come and take me away,
                 well, that's it. There is nothing I can do
                 about it. Worrying about it doesn't do
                 any good, so all I can do is keep work-
                 ing and if I can save up the money, then
                 pay them off. But until then, it's just
                 now and here, and it doesn't do any
                 good.

AS   83. ER: You do hope to pay them off.

OPIN,   84. EE: Well, yeah, I don't especially want to   3a
 FEEL   spend a couple of years in jail for bad
                 checks. However, at times when I'm
                 sleeping in my car on a cold night, it
                 does look kind of cheerful.

OPIN Q, 85. ER: Do you have any more specific plans
 CFQ,   for the future? I mean are you thinking
 DBL   of getting married or anything?
 BAR Q

OPIN   86. EE: No, I got a little growing up to do be-   3b
                 fore I can think about getting married.
                 It's not that I'm, I guess I am, act a lit-
                 tle younger than my age, but I really
                 don't care because I am 20 and I've got
                 a couple good years left in me anyway
                 and I just as soon doing a little more
                 running around anyway, so I'll just let
                 nature take its course on growing up
                 and keep on going. Oh, I mean, in Jan-
                 uary when things start going—I hope
                 start going a little better—I might
                 change my plans a little bit. But Jan-
                 uary is a month off yet, and a month

can be a long time, especially, living in a car.

LEAD (U) Q

87. ER: Don't you think your actions now are going to affect what you can do in the future, like your bad checks?

OPIN

88. EE: Yeah, but at the time I wrote these checks, I couldn't see any other way. I couldn't even draw any unemployment because the period now is the period I didn't make enough money.   2c

ENC, OPIN Q

89. ER: Uh huh. Do you have any specific goals, things that you want really bad?

OPIN

90. EE: A home. It's been quite a while since I've had a real home, and I'd kind of like to have one again.   3b

PROBE (OPIN) Q

91. ER: Have you any idea how you hope to set yourself up in a home again?

OPIN

92. EE: Oh, just in the normal way, start working. I've had kind of a bad outlook on work for a long time. Born naturally lazy. But like I say, I've got some growing up to do, and soon as I do that, then I can start living in a normal way, saving my money and the whole bit. People say everytime I see them, "Well, why don't you save your money?" Well, right now, I don't want to save my money, I want to have a good time, and I can't . . . the kind of good time I want is not the kind of good time you can have when you are married and trying to make a home and right now, I want it and if I don't do it now, I'll want it later . . .   3b

ENC	93. ER:	Uh huh . . .
OPIN	94. EE:	I mean, that's the way I see it, so I may 4a as well do it now and get it over with, and then I can start working . . .
I, AS	95. ER:	So to speak, sow your oats . . .
I, OPIN	96. EE:	. . . on my goals in life. Yeah, I was 4c endowed with a pretty large bag of wild oats. And it doesn't seem to be getting that much smaller right now.
PROBE (OPIN) Q	97. ER:	Well, when do you plan to settle down?
OPIN, NV	98. EE:	That's like saying, when's the wind go- 4c ing to stop blowing? I don't know, I mean, whenever I, it's something that just goes along, eventually you get tired of running around and start doing things differently, at least, that's the way I hope it works (*laughs*). I think my attitude will change, after I've decided I've had enough of sleeping in cars and two-bit apartments, and want to start getting something a little bit better out of it. It's not that I don't want these things now, it's just that I get a pay- check, and can see what I want, but it seems so far off; I can see here and now what I can do with that $100 or what- ever it is and I'll do what I can do now and I'll get later when it comes, when I get tired of doing this, that's just the way I work, er, think and act.
LEAD (I) Q	99. ER:	Does it look that far off to you?
OPIN	100. EE:	Yeah, things always look a long way 4a off, when you get—I don't know—it's

		like anybody else, when you first start something it looks like it will never end. My problem, I just won't start . . .	
ENC	101. ER:	Uh huh . . .	
OPIN	102. EE:	. . . If I start something, I'll be alright. That's why I think I'll eventually pan out into some sort of a normal human being. If I just once start it, I'm a bad starter at things.	4a
LEAD (I) Q	103. ER:	Don't you consider yourself a normal human being right now?	
OPIN	104. EE:	Well, in some respects, I mean I talk the same way as everybody else, but I, ah, no, I don't really. I mean I don't know of anybody else that acts the way I, I probably am. I mean I've never considered myself normal. Other people if they got evicted and they had to live in a car for a week, they'd probably break some kind of a record finding some place to sleep and hang their hat, whereas with me as long as I'm getting a meal at least once every other day, I figure I'm going to make it for a while anyway. I don't think that's nor-	2c
OPIN Q, LEAD (I) Q, DBL BAR Q	105. ER:	mal. Have you thought about doing anything about it? Are you just going to let it ride?	
I, OPIN	106. EE:	. . . Well, that's not . . .	
I, LEAD (I) Q	107. ER:	. . . Take things as they come?	
OPIN	108. EE:	Yeah, that's not really "let it ride." I'm doing something about it, actually, but I'm just not breaking my neck to do it. Things are working out alright, I mean,	2c

I'm working now. I've got a job that will last until I can get a better one when I turn 21 this January, and there's no big rush. I mean I'm not infringing on anybody else by not living somewhere and the only person's getting hurt out of the whole thing is me and I don't think I'm getting hurt that bad.

ENC   109. ER: Uh huh.

OPIN   110. EE: I mean I'm not the kind of guy that   3f
figures the world owes me a living so I'll just wait until it gives it to me. I realize I gotta work for it, but I got a lot of living to do yet. I mean I'll get it   2c
eventually, it's . . . it's just like, I mean, I don't worry about it.

PROJ Q   111. ER: How do people react to you when they first meet you?

OPIN   112. EE: I seem to set an impression on people;   1c
they think I'm intelligent, which I'm not.

PROBE   113. ER: What makes you think you're not?
(OPIN)
Q

OPIN   114. EE: Well, if I was intelligent, I wouldn't be   3f
running around sleeping in my car. I mean, it's not that I'm not intelligent. It's just that I don't try to be. I don't use my head. Of course, people seem to think I'm a real swift kid when they first meet me.

PROBE   115. ER: How about on the second or third
(OPIN)   meetings?
Q

OPIN   116. EE: They start realizing I'm somewhat of a   1c
clown and I really don't know, I'm not the kind of person who can talk to

somebody and find out what they're thinking. I wonder what they say behind my back, but I can never guess. I always think it's the worst, and as long as I think it's the worst . . . I'm just not the kind of person who can tell what somebody thinks about me.

GUG, PROBE (OPIN) Q	117. ER:	Um humm . . . how do you think about yourself?
OPIN	118. EE:	Oh, I think I'm not quite normal and a little underdeveloped in the head at times.	1c
AS	119. ER:	You know it's interesting because you said yourself that you have a job that requires, you said foreman, which seems to be a job with some responsibility.
AGR	120. EE:	Yeah.
OPIN Q, LEAD (U) Q, DBL BAR Q	121. ER:	How do you cope with this? Do you have any problems with this job?
DESC (FACT), OPIN	122. EE:	No. My boss will give me an order and he'll tell me which truck is coming when and when it comes, I get the truck loaded and get it out of the way, and if the truck doesn't come in then it's my duty to find out why not, and when it's gonna get there and to get it there, if it's anywhere possible.	1a
FACT Q	123. ER:	Do you have men working under you?
FACT	124. EE:	Yeah, I usually have about three; two or three.	1a

PROBE   125. ER: How do they react to you?
(OPIN)
Q

OPIN   126. EE: Well, they get the work done, so I guess   2b
I'm doing alright. I mean I haven't had
any bitches so far. We get along alright.
I don't push them and they don't mess
around with me. I'm generally pretty
easy to get along with. I carry a short
stick sometimes.

OPIN Q   127. ER: What credits do you give to yourself?

OPIN   128. EE: Well, I try to be congenial. I'm a pretty   1c
good drinker. There is nothing as far as
I can tell that I've got that is an actual
asset. All I've got is deficits. I realize   3f
everybody's got some assets some-
where, but I haven't been able to find
any.

ENC   129. ER: Uh huh.

OPIN,   130. EE: A long time ago I figured out to like   1c
FEEL   people, you don't see what's wrong with
them, but you look for the good, so
when I meet people, I start picking up
the things I like. But when I'm looking
at myself, I'm just the opposite. I try
very hard to hate myself, at least that is
the way it seems, and I have so many
things I lack in that they kind of over-
shadow the things that I do or don't
lack in, and these get kind of pushed off
back somewhere and there's all these
things: you're dumb, stupid, ignorant,
a clod. You don't know how to talk to
people, so that type of thing, you're
lazy. I don't even know what assets I

		have because I'm always picking myself apart with the things I don't have.	
LEAD (I) Q	131. ER:	Do you try and correct these?	
FACT, OPIN	132. EE:	That's one of my big things. I'll sit there, "you're doing this wrong, here's how you can do it right." And the next day, I'll go out and do it the same way I did it the day before. I'm also lazy. I don't care what it is, if you say "ain't" and you know it should be isn't it's a strain of some sort to stop and correct yourself. No matter how small it is, you can't just stop and start again the right way and once you fall into that thing you're doing wrong, saying "ain't," you subconsciously keep saying it.	4a
ADV	133. ER:	I think they call that self-discipline.	
AGR, OPIN, FACT	134. EE:	Well, that's it, yeah. But you have to stop yourself. With anything else, if I do it wrong, it's easier to keep doing it wrong. So I just keep on doing it wrong. Somethings, I don't say "ain't" anymore; but I still say "you-all."	
LEAD (I) Q	135. ER:	When you settle down, as you plan to do, do you hope to change these things then?	
DESC (FACT, OPIN, FEEL)	136. EE:	Well, before I can settle down and start . . . well, they'll have to be changed because the things I do, I can't both have a home and a successful life with the mistakes I do make. I have corrected some, I mean there are some things I've done wrong, and continually do wrong,	

and continually pointed them out to myself, and continually done wrong. But I have actually somewhat stopped, at least now, when I don't want to come to work, I come to work anyway, usually. And when something used to go wrong, I'd get real depressed so I'd sit there and cry to myself, you know . . .

ENC   137. ER: Uh huh . . .

DESC   138. EE: . . . sit there and think about how bad
(FACT,   things were going. Well, anymore, I've
OPIN,   stopped that. I don't correct it, but I'm
FEEL)   doing better than I was. At least I don't
     sit there and let myself get depressed. I
     change the subject or I do something so
     I won't sit there and get depressed
     about it, and although it's not the right
     way to go about it, when the depression
     goes away, I can at least see there's an
     answer, and through a crooked path,
     you know . . .

ENC   139. ER: Uh huh . . .

DESC   140. EE: . . . correct it. But I still don't . . . when
FACT,   I make mistakes when something does
OPIN)   go wrong, instead of moving to go fix it,
     I'll still sit there and hem and haw
     around and eventually get moving un-
     til I'll finally hit on the right course.

GUG,   141. ER: Uh huh. Do you get depressed often?
PROBE
(OPIN)
Q

OPIN   142. EE: Yeah, I did. I'm not as bad now as I
     used to be.

PROBE   143. ER: What depresses you most?
(FEEL)
Q

DESC   144. EE: Oh, it's just if I'm out of work, out of   1c
(FEEL,   money, and mainly hungry, and things
OPIN)   just generally aren't going right, I start,
boy, what a black ol' world this is and I
wished I'd died sometimes. Although I
don't have any serious thoughts about
killing myself. One of my other faults is
being cowardly.

AS, RAP 145. ER: That's not cowardly, I think.

OPIN,   146. EE: Well, I've given that a lot of thought,   1c
FEEL   and they say that somebody who com-
mits suicide is a coward, and they're
right. The only reason a person com-
mits suicide is because he can't put up
with life. It takes a lot of guts, though,
to put a gun to your head and pull that
trigger. It's easy to put the gun to your
head, but to pull the trigger, he's not
entirely a coward. I mean there's got to
be a little nerve there somewhere. And
I'm just flat a coward. I think about
suicide and I'm afraid to pull the trigger.

RAP   147. ER: Thanks a lot, Jim. That's the end.

III. Manifest content analysis

A. EE inputs

Under each subtopic in the interview plan, given are (1) the EE input numbers related to that subtopic; (2) a summary of the data obtained on the subtopic; and (3) an evaluation of the adequacy of the data collected, including description of data missing.

Jim's description of his present work situation (1a)

1. *EE inputs on this subtopic.* 4, 6, 122, 124.

2. *Summary.* Jim says he is now a foreman (6) over two or three men (124) in charge of loading trucks and boxcars in an onion shed (6) in Somersville (4). He is responsible for seeing that trucks are loaded as promptly as possible, upon being told by his boss when a truck is due (122).

3. *Evaluation.* The four EE inputs about Jim's present work identify the location and Jim's general responsibilities. We do not know (1) how long he has been working there; (2) how Jim reacts to specific conditions on the job; (3) what kind of relationship Jim has with his boss. With this much data missing, little can be inferred for the output.

Jim's description of his present financial situation (1b)   SKIP

1. *EE inputs on this subtopic.* 46, 48, 54, 72.

2. *Summary.* Jim reports he owes money on a car (46), some back rent (48), and some bad checks (48). He was evicted by his landlady (54). He is indefinite about the total amount of bad checks: about 15 averaging four, five, six dollars each (72).

3. *Evaluation.* The four EE inputs about the specifics of his present finances are too scanty. We need to know (1) the status of his indebtedness on his car, (2) the exact amounts of the bad checks, (3) perhaps more specifics about the back rent due, and (4) if there are other debts—such as to relatives—outstanding. Since EE generally was evasive about the realities of his financial problems, we are far from knowing how big the problems are.

Jim's description of his present personal adjustment (1c)

1. *EE inputs on these subtopics*
    (a) *Living arrangements.* 52, 76.

(b) *How he solves problems.* 56, 81, 82, 96, 98, 132, 134.

(c) *His self-concept.* 112, 114, 116, 118, 128, 130, 132, 146.

2. *Summary*

(a) *Living arrangements.* Jim reports he is living in his car (52, 76).

(b) *How he solves problems.* Jim reports he finds it difficult to keep concentrating on his main adjustment problems (56, 82) and tends to project blame on others or laugh them off (56). He states he does not worry about his debt problems, possible run-ins with police (81), and other people generally (56, 82). While he recognizes his mistakes, he finds he usually keeps doing things the wrong way (132–134). He reports he has a strong "here and now" attitude about his income. He spends his paychecks on immediate gratifications (96–98).

(c) *Jim's self-concept.* He has a very negative self-concept. He reports he tries to find likable qualities in others, but when looking at himself, he hates himself: he thinks he is dumb, stupid, ignorant, a clod and lazy (130–132). The only positive assets he listed were congeniality and being a good drinker (128). While others may initially think he is intelligent (112), he states he is not using his intelligence (114, 118, 128). He also thinks he is cowardly (146). He is so ensnarled in his negative self-image that he is unable to absorb feedback from others about his qualities—he said, "I'm just not the kind of person who can tell what somebody thinks about me" (116). He said he always thinks others "think the worst" of him (116).

3. *Evaluation.* The 17 EE inputs give us a fairly detailed, consistent picture of how EE is adjusting. These data appear usable for outputs.

Jim's description of his present social relationships (1d)   SKIP

1. *EE inputs on this subtopic.* 58, 112, 114, 116.

2. *Summary.* Jim thinks he makes a positive first impression on others: they think he is intelligent (112); a "real swift kid" (114). Asked further about how others react to him, Jim seems unable to report others' impressions—he shifted to talking about his own negative self-image (116). He said he doesn't worry about others (58).

3. *Evalution.* Data are too scanty here. ER only asked two questions. We do not know much about the kinds of relationships Jim has. Jim's negative self-image may make his social relationships very

meagre—but we cannot make this conclusion without some probing in the area of his social relationships.

Jim's description of his present relations with relatives (1e)
1. *EE inputs on this subtopic.* 60, 62, 64, 68, 78.
2. *Summary.* Jim reports his mother is dead, and his father is mentally ill (60). He said his father does not recognize him (60). He described an "ordinary" relationship with his siblings (62, 64). He stayed with an older brother on and off for about a year (78), and reports mixed feelings about being dependent on him (78). He says he has not revealed his financial problems to his siblings (68).
3. *Evaluation.* Data here are too scanty. Missing is (1) how does Jim react when father fails to recognize him?; (2) what specific circumstances led Jim to leave his older brother's home "for good"?; (3) more specifics about the kind and frequency of contacts with his siblings. We cannot draw conclusions here about sources of support or conflict for Jim's present and future adjustment.

Jim's perceptions of the satisfactions/dissatisfactions he now experiences (2b)
1. *EE inputs on this subtopic.* 8, 10, 56, 82, 98.
2. *Summary.* He does not like the kind of work he is now doing, nor the hours (8, 10). Throughout his descriptions of his present situation, he seemed to have no real strong satisfactions or dissatisfactions. He said, in effect, he is deferring long-term goals in order to gain immediate satisfactions (56, 82, 98). But he does not seem to be gaining strong positive rewards from his present pattern of behavior.
3. *Evaluation.* Based on information from 1c above, it appears the one conclusion stated in the summary is reliable. This conclusion should be stated with caution, however, because EE always chose to ruminate about his inner emotional state rather than the specific conditions under which he is functioning. If we needed to know the specific positive and negative reinforcers in his environment, we would need much more data.

Jim's ideas about reasons or causes for his satisfactions/dissatisfactions (2b)
1. *EE inputs on these subtopics*
   (a) *Dissatisfaction with work.* 16, 126.
   (b) *Causes of his evictions.* 56, 80.

(c) *Causes in Jim*. 98, 100, 102, 130, 132, 134, 136, 138.

2. *Summary*

(a) *Dissatisfaction with work*. Jim states he doesn't like his present job because the people are too "simple" and represent a life he rejects (16). Note, however, he states his subordinates get their work done and he gets along all right with them (126).

(b) *Causes of his eviction*. He admits he scapegoats his landlady for evicting him, but he does admit the eviction is really his fault (56). Repeating the topic later in the interview, he does express anger toward his landlady for not leaving him a warning note (80).

(c) *Causes Jim sees in himself*. Jim finds he cannot translate his worry about his problem into positive action. He finds he has great difficulty getting started to do something about his problems and his long-term goals (100–102). He believes he is very weak in overcoming his subconscious habits (130–136). Jim feels swept along by his absorption in immediate goals—he says he may change when he gets tired of running around, but he is as unpredictable as the wind (98). He thinks he has made a little progress (136–138). In general, it appears his negative self-image prevents him from solving his problems.

3. *Evaluation*. This question calls for a higher level of inference than any previous one. Data about Jim's environment are too scanty to be reliable. Data about Jim's own inner state appear adequate *per se* but we do not know how Jim sees the environmental causal factors interacting with his inner weaknesses and strengths. Therefore, we cannot draw very firm output conclusions on this subject.

Jim's perceptions of how he reacts to his usual pattern of functioning (2c)

1. *EE inputs on this subtopic*. 56, 81, 84, 88, 104, 108.

2. *Summary*. He finds he cannot keep focused on his real problems—he tends to deflect his worrying to something "unimportant" (56). In regard to the bad checks, he could not see any other way to keep from being hungry (88), and denies any future problems at times (81); at other times, being jailed might be a relief (84). In general, he thinks he is not functioning normally (104), but is not hurting himself too badly (108).

3. *Evaluation*. As with 1c, the data for 2c appear adequate. More probing to test the contradictions he expressed in terms of mixed feelings would help document the picture more fully.

Jim's description of his immediate goals (3a)
1. *EE inputs on these subtopics*
   (a) *Work.* 12, 14, 38, 44.
   (b) *Finances.* 74, 84.
   (c) *Personal.* 86, 92, 96.
2. *Summary*
   (a) *Work.* Jim plans to go to work for Jones' Delivery in a month (12–14). He thinks he will like driving professionally (38). He has no apparent concept of what advancement he might qualify for (44).

   (b) *Finances.* He has no specific plan for paying off the bad checks (74, 84).

   (c) *Personal.* He sees his present and immediate future consisting of "growing up" experiences (86, 92) which he describes as "running around . . . let nature take its course . . ." (86), or (ER's term) sowing some wild oats (96).
3. *Evaluation.* ER appears to have probed adequately in this area.

Jim's description of his long-term goals (3b)
1. *EE inputs in this subtopic.* 86, 90.
2. *Summary.* Jim sees marriage as a long way in the future (86). Jim would like a home—a real home (90).
3. *Evaluation.* EE input 90 gives a start, but we do not know how fully EE has developed his concepts. It is possible that EE, in another part of the interview (16), decries others at work who have a similar goal. We do not know the importance of this long-term goal.

Jim's description of what helps him reach his goals (3c)
1. *EE inputs on these subtopics*
   (a) *Work.* 40, 108, 136.
   (b) *Personal.* 138, 140.
2. *Summary*
   (a) *Work.* Jim thinks he will succeed at the new job in a month because he can put out more effort and do extra work (40). He seems to think being age 21 will make a difference in getting a "better" job (108). He says he now goes to work even if he does not want to; he is depressed less often (136).

   (b) *Personal.* He reports he has more control recently over his depressions, and feels more positively (138–140).
3. *Evaluation.* Again, data about Jim's inner state are fairly ade-

quate, but we do not know what Jim does when interacting with others.

Jim's description of what hinders him in reaching his goals (3d)
   1. *EE inputs on these subtopics*
      (a) *Conflict between immediate and long-term goals.* 48, 92, 94.
      (b) *Preoccupied with immediate goals.* 74, 86, 104, 136.
   2. *Summary*
      (a) *Conflict between immediate and long-term goals.* Jim thinks he cannot stop working to get schooling because he needs the income (48). He wants to do some "growing up" before he starts living normally (92–94).
      (b) *Preoccupation with immediate goals.* Jim repeatedly states he is so caught up in his immediate circumstances he cannot think of the future. He realizes he cannot have a home, a successful life with the mistakes he makes (136). He cannot think of the future even a month away (74, 86). He believes his motivation is not "normal," since he is satisfied with "getting a meal . . . every other day" (104).
   3. *Evaluation.* Again, data about Jim's inner state are fairly adequate, but we do not know what Jim does when interacting with others.

Jim's description of how much help/hindrance he gets from others (3e) SKIP
   1. *EE inputs on these subtopics*
      (a) *Unfair evaluation.* 22, 24, 32.
      (b) *Competition with work peers.* 40.
      (c) *Relatives.* 78.
   2. *Summary*
      (a) *Unfair evaluation.* Jim reports two cases of unfair judgment of his work (22, 24, 32).
      (b) *Competition with work peers.* Jim thinks he can surpass the reputed mediocrity of the other men working at Jones' Delivery (40).
      (c) *Relatives.* Jim does not expect to ask his relatives for further help (78).
   3. *Evaluation.* This is the weakest part of the interview, as indicated in 3c and 3d.

Jim's description of how much help/hindrance he is to himself (3f)
   1. *EE inputs on these subtopics*
      (a) *His ability to work.* 28, 34, 40, 136.

(b) *His initiative.* 84, 100, 102.

(c) *His intelligence.* 114.

2. *Summary*

(a) *His ability to work.* Jim knows he was not very reliable in the past (28). In the past, he says, he did the work he enjoyed, but slacked off if he did not like the work (34). He thinks he can put in extra effort and succeed (40). He says he now goes to work even if he does not want to (136).

(b) *His initiative.* He reports he is not a self-starter (100, 102). Sometimes, he feels like capitulating to the threat of being jailed (84).

(c) *His intelligence.* Jim thinks he is intelligent, but just does not use it (114).

3. *Evaluation.* We know quite adequately how negatively Jim evaluates himself. We do not know, however, what happens when Jim is interacting with others—there may be some relationships that spur him to be more positive. Conclusions here must be so qualified.

Jim's evaluation of what he would have to change in himself (4a)

1. *EE inputs on this subtopic.* 92, 94, 100, 102, 132, 134, 136.

2. *Summary.* He thinks he would have to give up having a good time in order to be married and have a home (92–94). He would have to become a self-starter (100, 102). He would have to be stronger in stopping himself from making repeated mistakes (132–136).

3. *Evaluation.* We face the same situation here as in subject area 3 above. We may draw some conclusions about Jim's inner states, but we do not know how contributory others may be in helping Jim to change.

Jim's evaluation of what others would have to change (4b)   SKIP

No data obtained on this subtopic.

How likely does Jim think he is to change himself? (4c)

1. *EE inputs on these subtopics*

(a) *Absorption with immediate goals.* 96, 98.

(b) *Improvements already made.* 138, 140.

2. *Summary*

(a) *Absorption with immediate goals.* Jim reports that his "large bag of wild oats ... doesn't seem to ge getting ... smaller right now" (96). He states, "eventually you get tired of running around and start doing things differently ... that's the way I hope it works" (98). He generally reports he finds the immediate here-and-now a more powerful incentive than the distant goals (98).

(b) *Improvements already made.* Somewhat more positively, he says he is doing better at getting to work and controlling his depressions (138). He does not say with any precision how he thinks he will accomplish further changes: ". . . eventually get moving until I'll finally hit on the right course" (140).

3. *Evaluation.* We face the same situation as in subject area 3 above. We may draw some conclusions about Jim's inner states, but we do not know how contributory others may be in helping Jim to change.

How likely does Jim think others are to change? (4d)
No data obtained.

Following are new topics introduced during the interview.

Jim's description of his past work experiences (5a)
1. *EE inputs on this subtopic.* 18, 30, 34.
2. *Summary.* Jim has driven a tractor, driven a forklift in a lumber mill, dug tunnels, run a boring machine for Hernandez Road Boring, and worked on a tugboat and as a farm laborer (18). He does not appear to have worked steadily (30, 34).
3. *Evaluation.* See the composite evaluation for nos. 5 and 6.

Jim's description of his past financial experiences (5b)
1. *EE input on this subtopic.* 50.
2. *Summary.* Jim said he cashed the bad checks so he could eat (50).
3. *Evaluation.* See composite evaluation for nos. 5 and 6 at end of section.

Jim's perceptions of his past satisfactions/dissatisfactions (6a)
1. *EE inputs on this subtopic.* 20, 26, 34.
2. *Summary.* Jim said he liked working on tugboats (20). He did not like working at the mill (26). He did not like working in the yard at Hernandez (34).
3. *Evaluation.* See composite evaluation for nos. 5 and 6 at end of section.

Jim's ideas about reasons or causes for his past satisfactions/dissatisfactions (6b)
1. *EE inputs on these subtopics*

(a) *Work.* 24, 32.

(b) *Finances.* 50, 88.

2. *Summary*

(a) *Work.* He thinks he was fired from working on tugboats because one of his bosses thought Jim "... wasn't his type..." (24). He "goofed off" at Hernandez, but was fired because his boss lost his temper (32).

(b) *Finances.* He wrote the checks not only because he was hungry (50), but also because he understood he could not draw unemployment (88).

3. *Evaluation.* See composite evaluation for nos. 5 and 6 at end of section.

Composite Evaluation (5 and 6)

Additional topics were added during the interview, but the questions were too scanty to give a reliable picture. In the initial plan, these topics were eliminated in order to keep the length of the interview to less than one hour. To cover them adequately, and perhaps gain much additional information, would take many more questions.

B. Outputs

These output conclusions are based on the analysis of EE inputs above. The numbers in parentheses refer to the subtopics in that analysis.

1. *Jim's self-concept.* Jim has a very negative self-concept: "dumb, stupid, ignorant, a clod, lazy, cowardly" are the words he uses (1c). He finds himself very weak in solving his problems. He tends to blame others, laugh them off, and remain preoccupied with his immediate gratifications (1c). His self-concept is so negative he cannot absorb feedback from others about his qualities (1c). He does not appear to be gaining strong positive rewards from his present pattern of behavior (he calls it "growing up" or "sowing wild oats") (2a), but is swept along by the incentives of his immediate goals (2b). He finds he has great difficulty getting started on his problems and long-term goals (2b). In the distant future are "normal" goals of marriage and a real home (3b). He thinks a new job that may open up next month will be a change for the better, but he has little concept of how to advance except by working harder than others (3a, 3c). Jim is so preoccupied with his immediate goals he cannot get started on longer-term goals (3d). He realizes he was unreliable in the past at work, but says he now goes to work even if he does not want to

(3f). He believes he really is intelligent, but does not use his ability.

The above conclusions appear to be adequately documented in the interview. Data were inadequate on planned topics 1b (finances), 1d (social relationships), 1e (relations with relatives), 3e (help/hindrance from others), and 4b (changes in others). On topics 2a, 2b, 3b, 3c, 3d, 3f, 4a, and 4c data were adequate in terms of descriptions of Jim's internal emotional states, but were inadequate in terms of how Jim actually sees himself functioning interpersonally. We do not know the degree to which Jim's actual functioning may alter as he interacts with others.

2. *Prognosis for Jim's future.* Jim appears to be set for continuing his laissez-faire approach to the problems he now has (4c). While he does report some positive improvements in his habits and control of his depressions (4c), his dominant preoccupation with immediate pursuits causes the writer to be quite pessimistic. Change may come from some external stimuli; there appear to be no inner stimuli strong enough to cause significant change.

Again, these conclusions must be considered tentative because we do not know Jim's strengths and weaknesses in actual interactions with others. With further interviewing, supplemented by observation of Jim in interpersonal situations, the writer could make more definitive conclusions.

IV. Commentary on critical interactions

This is a commentary on critical interactions that illustrate the especially good or poor communications in the interview. The criteria for effective logical and relational communication in Chapter 1 and the examples of nonverbal behaviors in Chapter 3 are used as a guide for selecting and commenting on the key interactions. For each key interaction selected, the commentary diagnoses the underlying logical and relational issues that appeared to be operating. For some of the poor examples, suggestions for better ER techniques are noted. Numbers refer to input numbers on the transcript.

Input number	Commentary
1	*Logical issue*. ER omitted ethics in discussion of PUR, and omitted TOPIC. ER explained his goal, but failed to explain the confidentiality of the interview and the topical goals for the EE. EE agreed to be interviewed—an action issue.
	Relational issue. ER stressed his goal and forgot to mention EE's goals because ER was worried about EE's willingness to get into his "problem" and EE's commitment (inclusion) to the interview. EE, however, showed his willingness to proceed.
3	*Logical issue*. ER's LEAD (I) Q and ABL BAR Q show his confusion and anxiety over the relational issue seen in input 1. Note ER's failure to start with a broad DESC Q, further showing he does not trust EE to give informative answers.
	Relational issue. ER was also feeling unsure of how well he could control EE, having already lost some control by starting the interview incorrectly. Thus far, EE appeared to be at ease, and gave ER exactly the information requested.

5   *Logical issue.* ER succeeded in asking a broader Q, and based it on a prior cue from EE. EE gave a relevant response.

     Relational issue. ER recovered some confidence in his ability to word questions, and has seen that EE is willing to cooperate. EE cooperated, and gave a longer answer.

9   *Logical issue.* EE showed NV FEEL in input 8. ER failed to use that cue. ER further limited potential EE response by asking a closed-ended OPIN Q which EE had already answered in input 8.

     Relational issue. ER was surprised by EE's NV FEEL input, and was unprepared to encourage EE to further express his feelings. A better Q would have been "Tell me what it's like, working ten to twelve hours a day."

11   *Logical issue.* ER changed the subject too soon, failing to get all relevant facts and opinions about EE's present work.

     Relational issue. ER still is moving away from EE's OPIN and FEEL cues. ER felt some dislike of EE here—EE appeared to feel uncommitted to his present work.

15   *Logical issue.* ER succeeded in getting back on the first topic.

     Relational issue. ER felt more confident, and asked a broad OPIN Q which EE answered cooperatively, in input 16.

17   *Logical issue.* ER changed the subject too soon. In input 16, EE has exposed a personal OPIN about the other people at work, which should be followed up as an indirect cue about his FEEL about himself. Change is too soon also because inadequate data have been obtained about his present work situation.

     Relational issue. ER felt dislike for EE, saw EE projecting his irresponsibility onto characteristics of other people. Having jumped to this conclusion, ER inadvertently went on to another topic without trying

to get confirmation of it because he disliked EE. ER
was influenced more by his feeling of dislike for EE
than by cues from EE.

21   *Logical issue*. After a productive OPIN Q in 19, and
an informative response from EE in 20, ER failed to
ask EE to describe his opinions further. Instead, ER
changed the subject and asked for an explanation of the
reason for changing jobs.

Relational issue. ER still is not listening to EE. ER
was convinced EE is irresponsible and disliked him.

25   *Logical issue*. Again, ER changed topic prematurely.
ER's AS would have been unnecessary if the questions
had developed more logically.

Relational issue. ER still felt dislike for EE, and was
trying to get EE to admit his lack of stability in his work.
ER felt that EE's response in 24 was a flippant rationalization. ER's AS conveys some disgust.

27   *Logical issue*. ER succeeded in asking a well-worded
question which flowed spontaneously from what EE had
just said.

Relational issue. ER felt more assured from EE's
response in 26. Note that EE in 28 showed more NV
FEEL.

29   *Logical issue*. ER probed for a FACT, missing the
other important FEEL cues in EE's 28.

Relational issue. As EE shows more FEEL, ER
backed off again with a FACT Q. EE's FEEL expressions
made ER uneasy. ER recovered in 31.

41, 43   *Logical issue*. ER asked good follow-up Q exposing
EE's lack of logical analysis of his situation showed in
his initial silence in 42, and his admission in 44 that he
does not know what he wants to advance to.

Relational issue. ER felt more confident here, in that
EE moved closer to his FEEL about others, compared to
the beginning of the interview. ER also felt assured
he had established EE's lack of foresight and planning

(although this needed to be done much more rigorously).

51   *Logical issue.* ER changed topic too soon.

    Relational issue. ER again backed off from cues given by EE because of his dislike for EE.

55   *Logical issue.* ER asked a good FEEL Q, following up on input 54.

    Relational issue. ER felt more trusting of EE, now that EE in 54 admitted to his present predicament.

59   *Logical issue.* ER got off the track by asking the reverse of what would be the next relevant question: "Please explain how your worrying about something unimportant, as you said a minute ago, connects with worrying about yourself too much." The DBL BAR Q shifted the focus to fact rather than continuing on with EE's feelings.

    Relational issue. ER was uneasy with EE's apparent lack of insight about his FEEL.

73   *Logical issue.* ER moved abruptly from FACT DESC to a question of EE's future action intentions.

    Relational issue. ER implied in the LEAD (U) Q that EE should be more responsible. In 74, EE partially agreed but appealed for ER's sympathy.

79   *Logical issue.* ER appeared more supportive of EE here. The LEAD (U) Q and DBL BAR Q indicated a shift of ER's opinion about EE.

    Relational issue. ER felt some empathy for EE's plight. EE has shown some responsiveness to ER's press for being more responsible; so now ER is showing more understanding of EE.

81   *Logical issue.* ER began with a good FEEL Q, but shifted to a LEAD (I) Q which put EE on the defensive in 82. EE's response was evasive, and repetitive of what he had already said in 56.

    Relational issue. ER mixed his empathy with his concern for EE becoming more mature. ER felt no empathy in 83, with a direct expression of ER's concern that EE pay off his bad debts.

89   *Logical issue.* ER posed a productive OPIN question, yielding the first definitive response from EE about his goals.

    Relational issue. ER felt more empathetic at this point, and continued with a good probe in 91. ER was more relaxed, willing to let EE speak. Note that ER's *first* ENC is in 89.

105   *Logical issue.* As in 81, ER shifted to questions of EE's future intent which made EE defensive.

    Relational issue. After a series of supportive questions, ER again expressed his concern over EE's irresponsibility.

111   *Logical issue.* A good use of a PROJ Q.

    Relational issue. ER was more at ease, and able to use an indirect question to help EE explore his self-concept. ER continued to show concern in 113, 115, and 117.

121   *Logical issue.* ER did well at probing about EE's work experiences.

    Relational issue. Following the successful questioning in 111–117, ER now had a more objective perspective on EE's behaviors and self-concept. ER was able to help EE express his opinions and feelings. ER continued successfully in 125, 127, and 129.

131   *Logical issue.* ER asked a LEAD (1) Q which EE had already answered; EE continued talk, however.

    Relational issue. ER shifted back to a more judgmental position, which shows more strongly in 133 and 135. EE became more compliant again.

141   *Logical issue.* ER has been ENC EE in 137 and 139, but now interrupts with a GUG and a limited OPIN Q.

    Relational issue. ER was anticipating the need to close the interview, but did not want to cut EE off abruptly.

147   *Logical issue.* ER cut off the interview very abruptly,
         after EE expressed strong personal feelings. Logically,
         ER should have gradually helped EE shift to a less per-
         sonal level of communication before ending.
              Relational issue. ER has empathized with EE, but
         also is tired of listening to him. The mixed feelings made
         ER awkward in how to pull away. EE has been con-
         trolling the interview, with rambling, circumlocutory
         statements which took ER back and forth from disgust
         to empathy. EE appeared very involved, and seemed
         to enjoy the chance to express himself in such detail and
         in the ways he chose, uncontrolled by ER.

V. Effects of extrinsic influences

A. Agency limitations

As a student at a university, ER was expected to comply with general university regulations and with the expectations of the instructor of the course. In this interview, there did not appear to be any organizational limitations that were conflictual with the intended purposes of the practice interview. EE was cooperative when he learned ER was a student at a university.

B. ER and EE roles

ER is in a subordinate position as a student. He was expected to conform to several rules laid out by the instructor, including ethical rights of EE, to not attempt to deliberately alter EE's behavior or feelings, and to submit a detailed self-critique of the interview. As part of the requirements for a graded course in interviewing, ER was subject to a dual judgment process: that of the instructor, as well as his own ideas of what interviewing is and how it should be evaluated.

ER is relatively inexperienced in the world of work. Hence the subject matter of the interview was fairly novel, making it more difficult to anticipate how to proceed. Further, ER had never had prior experience with the type of EE he had, namely, a person with a history of poor work habits and alleged minor criminal behaviors.

EE is a volunteer, which gave him much latitude in how much he chose to cooperate. EE appeared to find the interview situation fairly comfortable and did try to cooperate (but ER's lack of skill, coupled with EE's personality, resulted in a relatively poor interview).

C. The physical setting

The interview was conducted in a closed lounge in ER's dormitory. The setting was comfortable (soft chairs) and quiet. No unexpected interruptions occurred. ER and EE were sitting in soft chairs, with the audio tape recorder on a nearby coffee table. ER and EE were sitting directly opposite each other, about five feet apart, with a coffee table beside the two chairs.

EE seemed ill at ease in the university setting. Before going to the interview room, he asked many questions about what goes on in a college and glanced uneasily around the campus and the dormitory.

At the beginning of the interview, ER was very uneasy. While he had set everything (room, recorder) up in advance so that he would not keep EE waiting, his mind drew a "blank" as he was preparing to begin the interview. ER also felt awkward when turning on the recorder. EE began to appear more at ease once seated in the interview room. EE did watch ER turn on the recorder, but it did not appear to bother him.

Although EE appeared a bit uneasy at first, ER took longer to become at ease than did EE. There appeared to be no lasting negative effects of the setting on either person. The comfortable chairs and the quiet room seemed to help.

VI. Evaluation of interview behaviors

A. The objective count
See the tabulation in Figure 3, pp. 97–98.

B. The logical process
What was ER's skill in the use of the logical process? What was the impact of EE's style of logical communication on ER? Using the results of the analyses of the manifest content, the categorization of inputs, the objective count, and the analysis of critical interactions, here are some conclusions.

1. *Ratios of* FACT, OPIN, FEEL *inputs.* The plan for this interview called for about an equal ratio of OPIN and FEEL interactions, with about 20 percent FACT to define the specifics of each topic. ER asked 15 FACT Qs, 46 OPIN Qs, and 3 FEEL Qs—21 percent, 66 percent, and 4 percent, respectively. The FACT percentage is close to that expected. The OPIN Qs were excessively high, with far too few FEEL Qs. FEEL information often was implied in the OPIN Qs, especially the LEAD Qs, but ER failed to probe enough to elicit specific FEEL statements from EE.

EE's ratios were 30 FACT, 56 OPIN, and 8 FEEL—43 percent, 81 percent, and 12 percent, respectively. Thus, EE communicated almost exclusively at the levels of FACT and OPIN, consonant with ER's pattern. With 33 percent of EE's inputs being mixed, however, EE was constantly shifting logical levels, which makes it difficult to infer what EE's real opinions and feelings were.

Compared to ER's ratios, EE emitted twice as many FACT inputs, a few more OPIN inputs, and twice as many FEEL inputs. This differential ratio, combined with EE's high percentage of mixed inputs, indicates a rather jerky, discontinuous interview.

2. *Probing and the use of EE cues.* ER asked 21 PROBE Qs out of a total of 70. A more skillful ER would have had about twice as many PROBE Qs. Most (24) of the probing was in the OPIN category, indicating that ER was more likely to try to focus on EE's opinions than EE's facts or feelings.

From the critique of the critical interactions, ER failed to probe because he changed the topic abruptly five times (ER inputs 11,

17, 25, 51, 147) and shifted the level of communication too quickly ten times (ER inputs 3, 9, 21, 29, 59, 73, 81, 105, 131, 141).

ER did show some ability to follow through on EE cues, by staying on the same topic and probing well (ER inputs 11, 15, 27, 41, 55, 89, 121).

3. *ER's ability to word and focus questions.* After some initial stumbling in the wording of questions, ER did well in the clarity of the questions he asked. While there were too many DBL BAR Qs, the eleven incidents were not severely damaging to EE's responses. Clarity is indicated by the occurrence of only two EE CFSs and no EE CFQs. The one ER ECHO is also a positive indicator of good ER control of his verbalizations.

This EE was fairly cooperative, and often gave informative responses even though ER tended to ask too many closed-ended questions.

At the beginning of the interview, ER used narrowly focused FACT and OPIN questions when these were not indicated. The first LEAD (I) Q in input 3 was premature. The second LEAD (I) Q in input 81 was not skillful in that it narrowed the communication too fast. The next two OPIN Qs, 89 and 91, were good attempts to draw out the more specific feeling tones of EE's previous inputs. The next two LEAD (I) Qs, inputs 99 and 103, were unskillful because they were almost like advice-giving. The LEAD (I) Qs, in input 131 again narrowed the communication too fast; ER should have used a broader PROBE (OPIN) Q first. The last LEAD (I) Q in input 135 is again more like advice-giving.

ER asked seven unskillful LEAD (U) Qs.

ER used one PROJ Q and no SUP Qs. ER was too busy trying to sort out the direct control of the interactions and did not think of using indirect methods. The one PROJ Q was effective.

4. *Conclusions from manifest content analysis.* In the original plan, there were 19 subtopics; four new subtopics were added during the interview. ER covered eight of the original 19 subtopics with some degree of adequacy; none of the new subtopics was fully explored. This performance falls well below an 80 percent criterion. EE was preoccupied with ruminations about his negative self-image, so ER was successful on those subtopics relating to EE's self-image. When ER tried to lead EE into other topics, EE tended to reiterate his common theme of depression and failure. Since ER used very

few FEEL QS, EE may have been induced by ER's failure to validate his feelings to continuously repeat himself.

C. The relational process

What was ER's skill in the use of the relational processes? What was the impact of EE's verbal and nonverbal style of relational communication on ER? Conclusions are drawn from data in the objective count, the categorization of inputs, the critique of critical interactions, and the above analysis of the logical process.

1. *ER's feedback to EE.* ER used no SUM or REFL to give feedback to EE.

ER used one CR EX Q in input 53; it was skillfully done to check about EE's owing back rent.

ER used two RAP statements at the end of the interview. He could have used several more. Those used at the end were not effective because the ending was too abrupt. ER did use eight verbalized ENCs, improving in the second half of the interview. The eight ENCs average about one per every nine EE inputs, not quite frequent enough to give EE adequate verbal feedback. Eye contact was more frequent in the second half.

While ER repeatedly was frustrated with EE's defensiveness and pessimistic self-ruminations, ER did not show a skill in explicitly giving EE feedback about their relationship.

ER made six AS and one ADV statement. As seen in the analysis of critical interactions, ER had a difficult time converting his dislike for EE into a facilitative channel for communication with EE. The AS and ADV verbally show ER's opinions about what EE is like and what EE should do. This was a major weakness throughout the interview.

2. *Control of the interview by pacing.* The 147 inputs divided by 65 minutes of interview time yield a per-minute input rate of about 2.3, which is within the desirable range. Hence, the rate of interaction and length of EE inputs was adequate in this interview.

ER used no CS or PS. This indicates ER was posing his next questions too fast. ER needs to develop a slower pacing by using CS.

ER had no ANTS, two GUGS, and three IS. EE had three IS. While low in number, the eight disruptive behaviors reflect uneven pacing.

Overall, the pace appears adequate but can be improved by using CS and reducing interruptive inputs.

3. *ER and EE styles of* NV *communication.* EE's main NV vocal behavior was a nervous laughter, which stopped about halfway through the interview. This indicates ER was helping EE to be somewhat more comfortable. Initially, this EE NV behavior was disruptive to ER. EE's other vocal features were difficult to read. He tended to have the same inflections and tonal qualities at all levels of expression.

EE's eye contact with ER was poor at the beginning, but soon improved as he seemed to get comfortable in the interview room. EE conveyed an interest in following ER's lead with the eye contact.

Both EE and ER were relatively immobile, in terms of body position, arm and hand gestures, and unrelated body movements. The stillness of these movements perhaps reflected a moderate level of tension which lasted throughout the interview.

EE's facial expressions were largely indirect. He sometimes smiled when he was expressing negative feelings about himself—almost pleading with ER to support him. He sometimes frowned when he talked about his goals, convening a desire not to talk about the positives in his life.

ER did not show tension by vocal NV expressions. While ER's voice initially was tense, higher pitched than normal, his voice became lower pitched, warmer, with well-modulated volume as the interview went on. ER has good voice quality, although this asset was not sufficient to compensate for some of the major lacks of skill noted in earlier parts of the analysis.

ER used numerous facial expressions to give EE additional feedback about his reactions to EE. ER used good eye contact throughout the interview. ER showed interest and empathy much of the time. But ER also showed dislike and disdain in his facial expressions when he was most affected by his dislike for EE. All of these facial expressions tended, however, to be direct rather than indirect.

4. *Summary: inclusion felt by ER and EE.* ER experienced a strong feeling of commitment initially, but was frequently discouraged by EE's answers, which ER construed as uninformative. Hence, ER wavered between high inclusion and moderate inclusion.

EE often appeared to feel included, because many of his responses were actually what ER asked for. EE's indirect nonverbal communications were distracting and conveyed an avoidance of involvement. Since ER was rather unskillful in drawing EE out, EE may have felt only halfway committed to the interview. EE was willing to expose himself up to a point—to the degree he apparently had already thought through his situation and problems—but was unwilling to think and feel more deeply. This conclusion must be tempered, however, by ER's lack of control of the interview.

5. *Summary: control processes.* ER lost control of the interview many times, by starting off incorrectly and by allowing EE to repeat himself and communicate at mixed levels. ER also evaded deeper personal expressions by EE, often failing to probe on FEEL cues EE gave.

EE appeared to feel inferior to ER, especially when he first arrived on campus. EE's verbal behavior was largely controlling, however, since it is doubtful if EE revealed anything he had not previously anticipated.

6. *Summary: affection felt by ER and EE.* EE gave ER very few cues about how much he liked or disliked ER. At times, EE appeared to be spontaneously enjoying the communication, but he also quickly retreated and became more distant.

ER switched back and forth from a strong dislike of EE and his apparent lack of responsibility, to a feeling of empathy—more like sorrow—for EE.

D. Balance between logical and relational processes

What was ER's skill in balancing the logical and relational processes? How well did EE balance the logical and relational issues, and what was the impact of EE's style on ER? How much did ER do to guide EE into a logical and relational balance that would accomplish the purposes of the interview?

1. *EE's logical and relational styles of communicating.* EE was highly preoccupied with an intermingled set of facts, opinions, and feelings centered around a very poor image of himself. EE refused to explore other topics in any depth, especially in relation to his interactions with significant other people in his environment. EE's strong preoccupation with a limited area of his experience made him very inflexible, both logically and relationally. EE seemed almost unaware of his own patterns of verbal and nonverbal communication. Yet his impact on ER dominated the interactions.

2. *ER's logical and relational styles of communicating.* ER did show a wide range of verbal and nonverbal behaviors throughout the interview, both skillful and unskillful. ER was strongly affected by

two negative feelings: fear of EE's lack of commitment to the interview and dislike of EE's lack of responsibility. While ER did overcome these feelings several times during the interview and made some logical progress, he let them regain control and could not constructively channel them into the logical and relational issues occurring in the interactions.

E. Summary of ER strengths and weaknesses

ER strengths

1. ER held to the main outline of the planned topic (III.A). ER did especially well in covering EE's personal adjustment and reactions to his problems (III.A and B).
2. ER asked an adequate percent of FACT Qs (VI.B.1).
3. ER did explain PUR (IV).
4. ER used one PROJ Q well (IV).
5. ER probed for OPIN (VI.B.2).
6. ER worded questions well (VI.B.3).
7. ER's overall pacing was adequate (VI.C.2).
8. ER had good voice quality (VI.C.3).
9. ER offered direct, communicative nonverbal expressions to EE (VI.C.3).

ER weaknesses

1. ER failed to cover adequately EE's interpersonal experiences. When ER added new topics, he failed to get enough data (III.A and B).
2. ER omitted a review of the ethics and the TOPIC (IV).
3. ER asked too many OPIN Qs and too few FEEL Qs (VI.B.1).
4. ER failed to disentangle EE's FEEL inputs from EE's many mixed inputs (VI.B.1).
5. ER did poorly in handling the flow of logical issues in the interview, failing to probe many times, and changing the topic too abruptly five times (VI.B.2).
6. ER needs more practice in use of indirect questions (VI.B.3).
7. ER used too many LEAD (U) Qs (VI.B.4).
8. ER needs extensive practice in giving feedback to EE, especially use of SUM, REFL, ENC, and RAP (VI.C.1).
9. ER used too much AS and ADV, reflecting his relational problems with EE (VI.C.1).
10. ER made questions too narrow, before asking broader questions (VI.B.3).

11. ER used LEAD (I) Q prematurely and implied he was giving advice (VI.B.3).
12. ER needs more practice in the use of CS and reduction of GUGS and IS (VI.C.2).
13. ER lost control of the interview many times (VI.C.5).
14. ER was sometimes incapacitated by a strong dislike of EE (VI.C.6).

ANNOTATED BIBLIOGRAPHY

CHAPTER 1

BALES, R. F. *Interaction process analysis*. Reading, Mass.: Addison-Wesley, 1950.

Bales posited the importance of both a social-emotional (relational) dimension and a task (logical) dimension, each measured by six observation categories. Each category is defined in terms of its potential contribution to solving a problem in the group. The emotional areas relate to a tension-reduction model, which is narrower in scope than Schutz's (1958) relational theory. The logical areas parallel the logical issues used in the present book.

SCHUTZ, W. C. *FIRO: A three-dimensional theory of interpersonal behavior*. New York: Holt, Rinehart & Winston, 1958.

Schutz's original explanation of the derivation of his interpersonal theory. Illustrates the use of his questionnaire, the FIRO-B (for fundamental interpersonal relations orientation—behavior) to test the utility of his three dimensions of inclusion, control, and affection.

SCHUTZ, W. C. *Joy*. New York: Grove Press, 1967.

Joy shows in rich clinical detail how Schutz's interpersonal theory applies to experiences clientele have in his workshops at Esalen. The theory is useful both to diagnose blocks to participation in groups and to self-understanding, and to create a situation that will diminish the block.

SULLIVAN, H. S. *The psychiatric interview.* New York: Norton, 1954.

Sullivan took a behavioral, functional approach to his study of the psychiatric interview. Using theories of subjective perception, interpersonal relations, and communication, he developed a profound understanding of the interview process, abnormalcy, and therapy. He was among the early leaders who stressed the value of sound and pictorial records.

SYDIAHA, D. Bales' interaction process analysis of personnel selection interviews. *Journal of Applied Psychology,* 45 (1961): 393–401.

How much of the decision in an employment interview is related to the interpersonal processes codable by an observer? In this study, interview protocols were coded into Bales' twelve categories, then correlated with the accept-reject decision of the interviewer. A total of 12 percent of the variance was accounted for by the multiple correlation, a statistically significant finding.

CHAPTER 2

GUNTHER, B. *Sense relaxation: Below your mind.* New York: Macmillan, 1968.

Sensory awareness training is invaluable for developing awareness of one's inner affective states. Gunther offers many techniques, both individual and collective, for improving the use of senses. The book is a work of art—both pictorially and poetically.

HITTLEMAN, R. *Guide to yoga meditation.* New York: Bantam, 1969.

Any person may gain value from the elementary forms of physical and meditative Yoga. Hittleman shows how to do Yoga warm-up exercises, stressing deep breathing, which helps you be more relaxed and aware. The meditation focuses on your here-and-now experience of stimuli in the environment and in yourself, and helps develop confidence in the significance of inner experiences.

MALAMUD, D. I., AND S. MACHOVER. *Toward self-understanding: Group techniques in self-confrontation.* Springfield, Ill.: Charles C Thomas, 1965.

Presents a wide variety of verbal and imaginal exercises for use in groups to enhance self-awareness.

PERLS, F., R. E. HEFFERLINE, AND P. GOODMAN. *Gestalt therapy*. New York: Dell, 1951.

Perls was the first therapist who explicitly articulated and integrated a theory of nonverbal behavior in his work and writings. He stressed understanding behavior in terms of a person's style of sensory input and his typical motoric responses. The theory and practice are both profound and immediate; they strike at the core dimensions of personality and give an immediate comprehension of it.

PFEIFFER, J. W., AND J. E. JONES. *A handbook of structured experiences for human relations training*. Vols. 1 and 2. Iowa City, Ia.: University Associates Press, 1969, 1970.

An excellent selection and convenient description of 48 structured exercises for use in sensitivity training, dealing with personal awareness, interpersonal skills, and group dynamics in terms both of verbal and nonverbal dimensions of experience.

RUESCH, J., AND W. KEES. *Nonverbal communication*. Berkeley: University of California Press, 1956.

A comprehensive and succinct overview and pictorial presentation of nonverbal communication. Points out a key characteristic of nonverbal events: they are analogic, whereas words may be either analogic (discursive) or digital (denotative). As analogic events, nonverbal communication then tends to have more impact than verbal communication. Further, nonverbal events have a more explicit and unchangeable relation to their temporal and spatial context than do verbal events. The book also elaborates on the nonverbal aspects of Sullivan's ideas of the development of psychopathology.

SCHEIN, E. H., AND W. G. BENNIS. *Personal and organizational change through group methods: The laboratory approach*. New York: John Wiley, 1965.

Explains the origins, learning principles, and procedures used in sensitivity training.

SCHUTZ, W. C. *Joy*. New York: Grove Press, 1967.

Presents a wide variety of techniques for increased individual and interpersonal functioning. Schutz has imaginatively interwoven his interpersonal theory with Perls' (1951) approach.

CHAPTER 3

ROLE-PLAYING AS A TRAINING TECHNIQUE

CORSINI, R. J., AND S. CARDONE. *Role-playing in psychotherapy: A manual.* Chicago: Aldine, 1966.

A well-written guide to the rationale and varieties of uses of role-playing. Relevant to any setting.

MAIER, N. R. F. *Supervisory and executive development.* New York: John Wiley, 1957.

A helpful compendium of problem situations for role-playing in industrial settings. Each role-play is introduced by some theoretical considerations, with complete instructions for each role, and suggestions for data to be observed.

MORENO, J. L., AND H. L. JENNINGS, Eds. *The sociometry reader.* New York: Free Press, 1960.

Sociometric theory and psychodrama techniques developed by Moreno have laid the foundation for the use of action techniques in clinical training, and in group therapy. The use of action and drama impels the awareness of nonverbal communication.

VIDEO TECHNIQUES

BERGER, M. M., Ed. *Videotape techniques in psychiatric training and treatment.* New York: Brunner/Mazel, 1970.

A statement of the confrontation rationale for the use of video in psychiatry. Articles deal largely with therapy. The most helpful sections, IV and V, deal with ethics and technical suggestions.

BAILEY, K. G., AND W. T. SOWDER, JR. Audiotape and videotape self-confrontation in psychotherapy. *Psychological Bulletin,* 74 (1970): 127–137.

A succinct review of the rationale of confrontation feedback techniques, and the related research. To date, adequate research on the practical and heuristic possibilities is not available. Extensive bibliography.

NONVERBAL COMMUNICATION—REVIEW OF RESEARCH

DUNCAN, S. Nonverbal communication. *Psychological Bulletin.* 72 (1969): 118–137.

In a comprehensive review of research findings in three major areas of nonverbal communication, Duncan is optimistic about the potential contributions. The three major areas are *kinesics,* or body motion—including gestures, facial cues, eye movement, and posture; *paralanguage*—including voice qualities, speech discontinuities, and nonlanguage sounds; and *proxemics,* which is the use of space and the distance involved in communication acts. Duncan believes several significant nonverbal dimensions have already been empirically established.

LINGUISTICS AND PARALINGUISTICS:
THE STRUCTURE AND FUNCTION OF LANGUAGE

DITTMAN, A. T., AND L. C. WYNNE. Linguistic techniques and the analysis of emotionality in interviews. *Journal of Abnormal and Social Psychology,* 63 (1961): 201–204.

Illustrates an approach to studying how the structure of language relates to the inferred emotionality in interview behaviors.

DUNCAN, S., L. N. RICE, AND J. M. BUTLER. Therapists' paralanguage in peak and poor psychotherapy hours. *Journal of Abnormal Psychology,* 73 (1968): 566–570.

This study found that paralinguistic therapist behaviors—such as speech discontinuities and nonlanguage sounds—increased in those portions of a therapy session rated as poor by the therapist.

GOLDMAN-EISLER, F. *Psycholinguistics: Experiments in spontaneous speech.* New York: Academic Press, 1968.

Goldman-Eisler is one of the major contributors to linguistic and paralinguistic theory and research. This book sums up her recent work, which has led into the study of relatively unstructured, or spontaneous, behavior.

McQUOWN, N. A., Ed. *Natural history of an interview.* New York: Grune & Stratton, 1969.

Another major contributor to linguistic and paralinguistic research, McQuown has inspired research into the highly discrete, minute details of the interview.

PITTENGER, R. E., C. F. HOCKETT, AND J. J. DANEHY. *The first five minutes.* Ithaca, N. Y.: Martineau, 1960.

In the McQuown (1969) tradition of microscopic interview analysis, this book is a study of the first five minutes of a tape of one of Gill, Newman, and Redlich's (1954) initial interviews.

Presents a coding scheme for linguistic and paralinguistic behaviors.

SCHEFLEN, A. E. *Stream and structure of communicational behavior.* Bloomington, Ind.: University of Indiana Press, 1969.

This book sums up much of Scheflen's work in linguistics, paralinguistics, and their application in psychiatry.

PARALINGUISTICS: VOICE QUALITY AND AFFECT

A number of researchers have pointed to the special role of voice quality in conveying the affect of the speaker. The studies below usually involve blanking out the verbal content of speech so that only the nonlinguistic features remain.

HARGREAVES, W. A., J. A. STARKWEATHER, AND K. H. BLACKER. Voice quality in depression. *Journal of Abnormal and Social Psychology,* 70 (1965): 219–220.

By using a highly precise voice spectrometer, which measures voice pitch and volume, these researchers have found reliable features of the paralinguistics of depressed patients.

KRAMER, E. Judgment of personal characteristics and emotions from nonverbal properties of speech. *Psychological Bulletin,* 60 (1963): 408–420.

This review of the literature found, as early as 1963, a significant trend in positive findings on the relationship between nonverbal variables and personal characteristics and emotions.

SOSKIN, W. F. Judgment of emotion in word-free voice-samples. *Journal of Communications,* 11 (1961): 73–80.

Soskin has shown that pitch is a reliable indicator of emotion.

STARKWEATHER, J. A. Content-free speech as a source of information about the speaker. *Journal of Abnormal and Social Psychology,* 52 (1956): 394–402.

Starkweather eliminated word content by the use of white noise. The remaining auditory data showed promise for evaluating the emotional state of the speech.

PARALINGUISTICS: DISCONTINUITIES

FELDSTEIN, S. Vocal patterning of emotional expression. In E. H. Masserman, Ed., *Science and psychoanalysis.* Vol. 7. New York: Grune & Stratton, 1964. Pp. 193–208.

Do different emotions engender different speech patterns? This study suggests an affirmative answer. Using thirty actors and actresses, who read a standard passage reflecting eight different emotional states, Feldstein found that highest in speech disturbances was nervousness, followed by fear. Lowest in disturbances were hate and anger. In a middle range were conversational expression, or neutral, and depression and sadness.

MAHL, G. F. Disturbances and silences in the patient's speech in psychotherapy. *Journal of Abnormal and Social Psychology*, 53 (1956): 1–15.

Mahl developed a Speech Disturbance Ratio, or the "non-ah Ratio," in which seven behaviors—sentence change, repetition, stutter, omission, sentence incompletion, tongue slips, and intruding incoherent sound—are summed and divided by the number of words spoken. He studied this ratio as an index of anxiety, since anxiety presumably affects nonlexical properties of speech more than lexical.

MAHL, G. F. On the use of "Ah" in spontaneous speech: Quantitative, developmental, characterological, situational, and linguistic aspects. Digest of paper read at American Psychological Association, 1958.

Is "ah"—and similar expressions (eh, uhm, uh)—a gauge of speech disturbance? Mahl has found that they are not related to anxiety in the speaker. He infers that they reflect the speaker's pause to think, and are a signal to the listener not to interrupt because he wants to say more.

MAHL, G. F. Exploring emotional states by content analyses. In I. Pool, Ed., *Trends in content analysis*. Urbana, Ill.: University of Illinois Press, 1959. Pp. 89–130.

Continuing the development of his "non-ah Ratio," Mahl found that disturbances are frequent. They occur on the average of one every 4.6 seconds, or every 16 words. Individual differences in rate are very apparent. A speaker is typically unaware of the kinds and amounts of his speech disturbances.

SCHULZE, G., G. F. MAHL, AND E. J. MURRAY. Speech disturbances and content analysis categories as indices of underlying emotional states of patients in psychotherapy. *American Psychologist*, 15 (1960): 405.

Are speech disturbances related to concurrent emotional content?

This study found that speech disturbances are unrelated to the manifest language content of speech of patients in therapy.

PARALINGUISTICS AND THE INTERACTION CHRONOGRAPH

The interaction chronograph was devised by Chapple (1949) to measure in split-second precision the duration of utterances and silences in communication. Programmatic research on these variables has been done by Goldman-Eisler (1968) as well as by the following.

CHAPPLE, E. D. The interaction chronograph: Its evolution and present application. *Personnel*, 25 (1949): 295–307.

Chapple assumes the key impact of communication is contained in the nonlinguistic variables of duration and rate of speech utterances, duration of silences, and the pattern of interruption of speech and breaking of silences. The promise of this assumption has led to major programmatic research.

JAFFE, J., AND S. FELDSTEIN. *Rhythms of dialogue.* New York: Academic Press, 1970.

Jaffe and Feldstein have fully automated the interaction chronograph, from initial sound input to data collation by a computer. They found that temporal patterns in unstructured dialogue show consistent regularity, and have developed a mathematical expression of the pattern. They found that some of the stability of the pattern is attributable to the personality of the speaker, while some is attributable to the social context. In spontaneous interchanges, they detected a strong tendency for both speakers to match the durations of each other's pauses, but no tendency for them to match the duration of vocalizations.

MATARAZZO, J. D. The interview. In B. B. Wolman, Ed., *Handbook of clinical psychology*. New York: McGraw-Hill, 1965. Pp. 403–450.

Using the interaction chronograph, and controlling the kinds and durations of interviewer behavior, Matarazzo and his colleagues at the University of Oregon Medical School have found significantly reliable and valid results. Duration of speech, under the usual conditions of a structured or semistructured appraisal interview, has been found to be a highly reliable behavior across many types of interviewees—both industrial applicants and clinical patients. When the interviewer speaks for less than five or ten seconds and is nondirective in approach, the ratio of interviewer-interviewee speech utterance approximates 1:5. Careful investigation of other possible factors (number of questions asked, open versus closed type questions, differential speech rate) ruled them out, leaving duration *per se* as the essential empirical variable. Further studies have defined some of the parameters of responses to silence—both reaction-time latency and initiative latency—and have shown correlations with age, IQ, socioeconomic status, and Taylor Anxiety Scale scores.

Validity studies have shown that sickest groups (schizophrenics) have the lowest duration scores, while normals have the highest. Further, in terms of the interviewer manipulating interviewee duration, both head-nodding and saying "mm-hmm" significantly increase it.

KINESICS: POSTURE AND BODY MOVEMENT

BIRDWHISTELL, R. L. Some relationships between American kinesics and spoken American English. In A. Smith, Ed., *Communication and culture*. New York: Holt, Rinehart & Winston, 1966.

Birdwhistell has had a major impact on research in kinesics and proxemics. Here, he elucidates the cultural norms in America for posture, gesturing, and their concurrence with verbalizations.

DITTMAN, A. T. The relationship between body movements and moods in interviews. *Journal of Consulting Psychology*, 26 (1962): 480.

While Dittman found that there may be significant individual differences in patterns of body movement, a given person moves in reliably different patterns as he experiences different moods.

DITTMAN, A. T., M. B. PARLOFF, AND D. S. BOOMER. Facial and bodily expression: A study of receptivity to emotional cues. *Psychiatry*, 28 (1965): 239–244.

Using clinicians and dancers as judges, this study compared the judges' sensitivity to face plus body (whole) versus body alone for pleasant and unpleasant nonverbal expressions. All judges gave facial expression more weight, although the dancers were more reliable on judging the affect in body alone, than were clinicians. All judges had adequate reliability on judging body alone without facial cues.

EKMAN, P. Body position, facial expression, and verbal behavior during interviews. *Journal of Abnormal and Social Psychology*, 48 (1964): 295–301.

How well correlated are verbal and nonverbal cues? In this study, untrained judges were able to accurately relate body position to the verbal content of interviews.

EKMAN, P., AND W. V. FRIESEN. Nonverbal behavior in psychotherapy research. In J. Shlien, Ed., *Research in psychotherapy*. Vol. 3. Washington, D.C.: American Psychological Association, 1968. Pp. 179–216.

These researchers corroborate the above studies showing distinct patterns of body motion for individual patients. Patterns also appear to be a function of the ongoing interpersonal relationship and defensive behaviors. Interested in the relations between body motion and emotionality, they have developed reliable schemas for coding body motion in four types: body acts, body positions, facial expressions, and orientation of the head.

EXLINE, R., D. GRAY, AND D. SCHUETTE. Visual behavior in a dyad as affected by interview content and sex of respondent. *Journal of Personality and Social Psychology*, 1 (1965): 201–209.

Eye contact has been singled out as an important variable in kinesics. This study explored several parameters of the occurrence of eye contact. Using a neutral and a potentially embarrasing interview, the occurrence of eye contact was investigated in terms of silent versus talking, female versus male interviewee, condition in the interview, and FIRO-B (Schutz, 1958) scores. The interviewees looked at the interviewer more when silent than when speaking. Female interviewees looked more than males. All subjects looked less when under the personal-embarrassing condition. Both female and male subjects who scored high in FIRO-B scales on inclusion and affection showed significantly more eye contact that those who scored low.

FRANK, R. L. Tactile communication. *Genetic Psychology Monographs*, 56 (1957): 209–255.

What is the significance of touching and being touched in interpersonal relations? This pioneering monograph outlines some of the potential significance of what is perhaps one of the most potent nonverbal behaviors. As an intimate form of action, its message is unavoidable.

SCHEFLEN, A. E. The significance of posture in communication systems. *Psychiatry*, 27 (1964): 316–331.

Scheflen outlines the cultural, group, and individual dimensions of posture. Scheflen takes the position that posture is not a personality quality, but rather is a group- or culture-determined behavior which serves to mark several structural features of the process of communication.

TAGUIRI, R. Person perception. In G. Lindzey and E. Aronson, Eds., *The handbook of social psychology*. 2nd ed. Vol. 3. Reading, Mass.: Addison-Wesley, 1969. Pp. 395–449.

Studies of judgments of facial expressions evolve into a six-step scale of ease (from high to low): love, happiness, mirth; surprise; fear and suffering; anger and determination; disgust; contempt. Emotions seen as opposites (for example, mirth–contempt) tend to be the most difficult to differentiate. The six-step scale of difficulty appears to have two underlying dimensions: pleasantness–unpleasantness and attention–rejection.

PROXEMICS: HOW SPACE AFFECTS INTERACTIONS

HALL, E. T. *The hidden dimension*. Garden City, N.Y.: Doubleday, 1966.

What difference do space and distance make in potential and actual verbal and nonverbal communications? This insightful study of proxemics suggests there are four significant distances in two-person configurations: intimate (up to 18 inches), casual-personal (18 to 48 inches), social-consultative (4 to 12 feet), and public (12 feet to maximum audible distance of the voice). The closer the distance, the closer the relationship the persons are experiencing. Functionally, the availability of information to receptor systems (visual, tactile, auditory, and olfactory) changes notably across the four different ranges, so that only certain kinds of information are usually transmitted within each category.

SOMMER, R. Small group ecology. *Psychological Bulletin*, 67 (1967): 145–152.

The ways people disperse themselves in a given space have been shown to be a function of four variables: the nature of the group task, the degree of relationship among the group members, the personalities of the group members, and the amount and kind of space available.

CHAPTER 4

EFFECTS OF THE INTERPERSONAL SITUATION:
ROLE, STATUS, PERSON PERCEPTION

A major theme emerging from research on the interview is that the givens of a specific interpersonal situation may determine more of what happens in the communication than the intrinsic qualities of the communication itself. By given is meant the personality and the cultural and social influences both the interviewer and the interviewee bring with them to the interview process.

BENNEY, M., D. RIESMAN, AND S. A. STAR. Age and sex in the interview. *American Journal of Sociology*, 62 (1956): 143–152.

Looking at the facilitation of communication when age and sex of the interviewer and respondent were systematically varied, this study found that communication was maximized when both were young and were of the same sex. Communication was least complete when both were of the same age (older or younger) and of the opposite sex.

COUCH, A., AND K. KENISTON. Yeasayers and naysayers: Agreeing response set as a personality variable. *Journal of Abnormal and Social Psychology*, 60 (1960): 151–174.

Prior to this research, interview trainers tended to assume that the leading question, or highly focused question, was more likely to be answered by the interviewee, regardless of his personality, in a socially acceptable direction. This research showed that some persons are "yeasayers," who have a strong response bias to say yes to questions.

LENSKI, G. E., AND J. C. LEGGETT. Caste, class, and deference in the research interview. *American Journal of Sociology*, 65 (1960): 463–467.

This study examines the operation of an acquiescence bias when interviewees are from a lower caste or class than the interviewer.

POPE, B., T. BLASS, J. A. CHEEK, AND A. W. SIEGMAN. Some effects of discrepant role expectations on interviewee verbal behavior in the initial interview. *Proceedings*, Seventy-eighth Annual Convention, American Psychological Association, 1970. Pp. 527–528.

When EEs experienced ER behavior quite different from what was expected, certain signs of stress in EE behavior did occur. EE productivity was less than in a comparable control group. There also was a decrease in resistiveness, defined as the avoidance of personal exposure, and a tendency for an increase in superficiality, a stronger avoidant response. While other predictions about fluency decreases did not occur, the results succeed in showing signs of stress in EE behavior due to discrepancies between their expectations and actual ER behavior.

SHRAUGER, S., and J. ALTROCCHI. The personality of the perceiver as a factor in person perception. *Psychological Bulletin*, 62 (1964): 289–308.

General factors such as accuracy or assumed similarity have produced unclear results. There is more promise in the research on specific descriptive dimensions. The most prominent feature of any description of a person has been found to be favorability. There are trends in the data showing that people who see themselves as hostile will ascribe hostility to others. Judges have a complex, somewhat novel multidimensional set of response biases.

SILVER, R. J. Effects of subject status and interviewer response program on subject self-disclosure in standardized interviews. *Proceedings*, Seventy-eighth Annual Convention, American Psychological Association, 1970. Pp. 539–540.

ER and EE status was varied in two ways: by pre-interview instructions, and by evaluative versus nonevaluative ER responses given at one-minute intervals in the 30-minute interviews. The highest self-disclosure occurred when ER was evaluative and EE was high in initial status. EEs experienced more comfort when their status was low and ER was nonevaluative.

TAGUIRI, R. Person perception. In G. Lindzey and E. Aronson, Eds., *The handbook of social psychology*. 2nd ed. Vol. 3. Reading, Mass.: Addison-Wesley, 1969. Pp. 395–449.

Taguiri does a comprehensive review of the characteristics and processes by which one person perceives or judges another. Much progress has been made in the complex research problems in person perception. Sound research in this area has to take into account the interplay between the judge, the stimulus person, the situation, the elements to be judged, and the procedures used. The stimulus person is always highly sensitive to situational cues.

It is now known that there are two kinds of accuracy in judging, which are independent of each other: the judgment of stereotypes, and the judgment of differential characteristics of an individual. Women have been found to have more tendency to stereotype than men, so the sex of the judge should always be taken into account.

The rest of the annotated bibliography for Chapter 4 consists of publications in specific applied areas. Cited are suggestions or guides for planning and conducting interviews, and research findings on the process and outcomes of interviewing as an assessment device.

CLINICAL: SOCIAL WORK, PSYCHIATRY, PSYCHOLOGY, COUNSELING

BURDOCK, E. I., AND A. S. HARDESTY. Structured clinical interview manual. New York: Springer-Verlag, 1969.

A carefully constructed, highly standardized interview, with a convenient recording format for the assessment of psychopathology. The manual includes both an interview protocol and an inventory of 179 verbal and nonverbal behavioral items for the interviewer to observe. Scored while conducting the 20-to-30-minute interview, pattern scores on ten subtests are derived. Examples of subtest scores are anger-hostility, conceptual dysfunction, fear-worry, physical complaints, self-depreciation, sexual problems. This highly structured approach has two important advantages in interviewing: first, the unreliability of the typical, less structured diagnostic interview should drop out; second, the dimensions scored are more relevant to formulation of treatment recommendations than the traditional diagnostic labels.

FENLASON, A. F., G. B. FERGUSON, AND A. C. ABRAHAMSON. *Essentials in interviewing: For the interviewer offering professional services.* Rev. ed. New York: Harper & Row, 1962.

Intended for an orientation to the social casework interview, and related professional interviewing. Stresses the importance of understanding the background of the individual client—his culture, his personality, and his roles—and how the dynamics of the interview may be used to help the agency solve relevant aspects of the client's problem. Emphasizes a nondirective style, and focuses more on how to infer the client's characteristics than on understanding the actual experience of the interview for both parties. Replete with actual examples of interviews and illustrations of inferences made by the authors.

GARRETT, A. *Interviewing: Its principles and methods*. New York: Family Service Association of America, 1970.

> Unhappily, Miss Garrett died before having a chance either to revise her classic text for social work teaching or to write a new book. The principles are fairly abstract, while the cases are presented in rich detail.

GILL, M., R. NEWMAN, AND F. C. REDLICH. *The initial interview in psychiatric practice*. New York: International Universities Press, 1954.

> After an informative overview of the major shifts in the rationale implied in the history of the psychiatric interview, the authors stress that the role of the interview has shifted from a fact-finding one to the diagnostic evaluation of the actual interpersonal relationship currently occurring between patient and therapist. Including audio records of three interviews, the book proceeds to outline in detail how the authors think a relationally oriented interview should be conducted. Theory used is psychoanalytic and Sullivanian. The detailed critique of interview dynamics is couched in terms of the therapist's rationale for each question asked (the therapist's own feelings are seldom reported), an analysis of the patient's dynamics, and occasional observations about how both seem to be feeling.

KANFER, F., AND G. SASLOW. Outline of interview information needed for a functional analysis. An addendum, unpublished, to Behavioral analysis: An alternative to diagnostic classification. *Archives of General Psychiatry*, 12 (1965): 529–538.

> Kanfer (an experimental psychologist) and Saslow (a psychiatrist) show how a developmental and learning approach to the purpose and outline of an assessment interview produce much more useful information than the traditional psychiatric intake exam, or mental status examination. The addendum is a specific, highly detailed outline of the major present and past areas of the patient's experience. Throughout, the focus is on the presenting problem, and how present and past experience reinforce the problem behaviors.

PETERSON, D. R. *The clinical study of social behavior*. New York: Appleton-Century-Crofts, 1968.

> When Peterson had a sabbatical year to review the research find-

ings on assessment in clinical psychology, he concluded that there was a need across all areas for a much more rigorous use of scientific methods. In relation to interviewing, he calls for a systematic study of the functions of the degree of structure of the interview; his hunch is that a moderate degree (a guided interview) is preferable. He suggests a guide for the clinical assessment interview, focusing on understanding the nature, severity, and determinants of a patient's problem behavior. He also emphasizes the relational quality of the interviewer-interviewee interactions. His recommendations are consistent with the functional analysis proposed by Kanfer and Saslow (1965).

RICH, J. *Interviewing children and adolescents*. London: Macmillan, 1968.
A practical guide to conducting different types of interviews with youngsters. Points out many specific ways in which communications with children differ from interactions with adults. The approach is eclectic, both behavioristic and psychoanalytical.

RICHARDSON, S. A., B. S. DOHRENWIND, AND D. KLEIN. *Interviewing, its forms and functions*. New York: Basic Books, 1965.
A highly informative account of the parameters and research on interview behaviors. Presents both a series of informative frameworks within which to view the behavioral, functional issues, and also cites findings of relevant empirical studies.

ROGERS, C. R. *Client-centered therapy*. Boston: Houghton Mifflin, 1951.
Rogers stresses the direct experience of interview interactions, and the role of interviewer as a facilitator for the interviewee to discover and clarify his phenomenal world. Known as the nondirective approach to therapy, many of the techniques, such as reflection and summarizing, are of essential value in depth interviewing.

RUESCH, J. *Therapeutic communication*. New York: Norton, 1961.
An excellent extension of Sullivan's approach. Especially useful is his summary of the principles of communication, pp. 451–467, and their relation to normal and abnormal behavior.

SAUL, L. J. The psychoanalytic diagnostic interview. *Psychoanalytic Quarterly*, 26 (1957): 76–90.

A comprehensive outline of the interpretive psychoanalytic interview, adaptable to nonanalytic frameworks. The schedule of questions is in three parts: anamnestic data—chief complaints, routine day, onset of symptoms, developmental and medical history; conscious attitudes—toward others, self, future, mental status, personality dynamics, strengths; and unconscious associative material—memories, dreams, fantasies, nonverbal expressions, indications of transference.

SPITZER, R. L., AND J. ENDICOTT. Diagno II: Further development in a computer program for psychiatric diagnosis. *American Journal of Psychiatry*, 125 (1969): 12–21.

Outlines a structured interview, called Current and Past Psychopathology Scales (CAPPS), for collection of 96 variables, including age, sex, and 94 scaled ratings made from the interview data. Uses a decision-tree model for the diagnostic decision-making process: 57 decision points are programmed, resulting in findings on 46 different diagnostic classifications in the Kraeplinian tradition.

STEVENSON, I. *The psychiatric examination*. Boston: Little, Brown, 1969.

After a one-chapter review of research on the reliability and validity of the psychiatric examination, the author devotes the remainder of the book to a traditional approach to purpose and procedures of the psychiatric examination. Offers detailed data on signs and symptoms and how they relate to traditional diagnostic categories.

SUNDBERG, N. D., AND L. E. TYLER. *Clinical psychology: An introduction to research and practice*. New York: Appleton-Century-Crofts, 1962.

A comprehensive survey of theory, research, and practice in assessment and therapy in clinical psychology. Chapter 4, pp. 77–101, gives an example of how information theory applies to the process of assessment. Chapter 4 also suggests a general topical guide for a complete case study, ranging from a present functioning, intrapsychic and interpersonal analysis, development, and diagnosis and recommendations. In Chapter 5, pp. 102–130, the situational, personal, and interactional facets of the interview are outlined. In Chapter 7, pp. 164–196, important stress is placed on understanding the person in the context of the situation of the interview.

WOLBERG, L. R. *The technique of psychotherapy.* 2nd ed. New York: Grune & Stratton, 1967.

In Part One, Wolberg suggests eight goals for the initial interview in psychotherapy: establish rapport; establish a tentative diagnosis, dynamics, and etiology; estimate assets and weaknesses; and make practical arrangements for therapy and other needed consultations. Rich in practical details. The appendix in Part Two gives a guide for the initial interview, corresponding to the eight goals suggested in Part One.

EDUCATION

LANGDON, G., AND I. W. STOUT. *Teacher-parent interviews.* Englewood Cliffs, N.J.: Prentice-Hall, 1954.

A persuasive presentation of the vital need for teachers to interview parents, and interview them well. Gives excellent practical guides for what to talk about, what situations call for an interview, what to expect and what information to try to get, what solutions a teacher may try, and what to do with special problems during the interview. Examples of content covered in actual interviews from kindergarten to high school are given. Provides detailed considerations for planning an interview. Ends with a short list of interviewing do's and don'ts.

SACHS, B. M., AND G. V. S. PITCOCK. *The student, the interview, and the curriculum.* Boston: Houghton Mifflin, 1966.

Taking the curriculum to mean the totality of the school environment, the authors illustrate how interviews elucidate the student's dynamics and the role of the counselor, teacher, and administrator in five interview transcripts. The commentaries speak more to broader issues of human problems and the connection with home and school experiences, than they do to interviewing techniques *per se.* It is a useful, thought-provoking documentary of how important it is to listen to what pupils are saying.

EXPERIMENTAL RESEARCH

MERTON, R. K., M. FISKE, AND P. L. KENDALL. *The focused interview: A manual of problems and procedures.* New York: Free Press, 1956.

This manual is a guide for postexperiment interviewing of subjects to ascertain their perceptions of the experiment. It is for use after subjects have gone through a known specific procedure, and the experimenter already has made some analysis of the data. Suggests relevant criteria and detailed ways to evaluate the subjects' responses.

INDUSTRIAL-GOVERNMENTAL

BINGHAM, W. V. D., B. V. MOORE, AND J. W. GUSTAD. *How to interview.* 4th ed. New York: Harper & Row, 1959.

The first two chapters of this standard reference on interviewing review some selected findings and issues in the research literature on interviewing and therapy. In Chapter 3, numerous guideposts are suggested for general interviewing, plus a separate section on interviewing for facts. Practical considerations and further guideposts for these specific uses of interviewing are given in the remainder of the book: employment, civil service oral exam, public opinion surveying, human relations problem-solving, journalism, legal and law enforcement, intake or case study, vocational counseling, and the clinical interview.

FEAR, R. A. *The evaluation interview: Predicting job performance in business and industry.* New York: McGraw-Hill, 1958.

Suggests a broad outline for a semistructured interview with strong emphasis on listening and nondirective skills on the part of the interviewer.

KRUG, R. E. Personnel selection. In B. von Haller Gilmer, Ed., *Industrial psychology.* 2nd ed. New York: McGraw-Hill, 1966. Pp. 140–166.

A useful, current summary of all phases of research needed to assess the value of predictions made from interviews and tests about the future job performance of applicants.

MCMURRY, R. N. Validating the patterned interview. *Personnel,* 23 (1947): 263–272.

McMurry was one of the first to suggest a more structured interview protocol. Along with the overt wording of questions, the schedule also (in lighter print) reminds the interviewer of the underlying intent of the question as an aid for probing.

MAIER, N. R. F. *The appraisal interview.* New York: John Wiley, 1958.

Through a detailed analysis of six role-played performance appraisal interviews, Maier insightfully demonstrates the interplay of objectives, methods, and skills involved. Three methods are compared: tell and sell, tell and listen, and a joint problem-solving approach.

MAYFIELD, E. C. The selection interview—a re-evaluation of published research. *Personnel Psychology*, 17 (1964): 239–260.

Updating Wagner's (1949) review of the research on the reliability and validity of the industrial selection interview, Mayfield drew about the same conclusions. Based on actual research findings, the extensive use of the interview should be seriously questioned. Research procedures vary too much to make studies comparable for generalization.

Findings tend to agree on some points. An interviewer appears to behave about the same across interviewees. Studies of skill training show that definitive differences in style do result. A general rating predicting suitability should not be used—it is rarely predictive. Some of the reliability problem appears to be due to the way interviewers differentially weight information (even if they have exactly the same data). Structured interviews yield higher inter-interviewer reliabilities. Even with higher reliabilities, however, interview predictions continue to yield low validities. The differential validity of an interview, when added to available test scores, tends to be zero, unless a team of interviewers is used for an amalgamated rating. The only trait reliably and validly estimated from interviews is intelligence: an expensive use of interview time. In the typical unstructured employment interview, the interviewee talks less than the interviewer.

SHOUKSMITH, G. *Assessment through interviewing.* Long Island City, N.Y.: Pergamon, 1968.

A cursory guide largely for industrial interviewing. Shows the practical use of both individual and group interviewing. Reports some validity data on the selection of airline pilots.

WAGNER, R. The employment interview: A critical summary. *Personnel Psychology*, 2 (1949): 17–46.

The first rigorous review and critique of the reliability and validity of the employment interview concludes that the interview is useless as a measure of personality and a predictor of job performance.

ULRICH, L., and D. TRUMBO. The selection interview since 1949. *Psychological Bulletin*, 63 (1965): 100–116.

This follow-up to Wagner's (1949) review drew essentially the same conclusions as did Mayfield (1964). All such reviews have stressed the potential merit of a higher degree of structure so that reliability might be increased. Yet unanswered in any research is how to increase validity.

NURSING

BERMOSK, L. S., AND M. J. MORDAN. *Interviewing in nursing*. New York: Macmillan, 1964.

An amalgamation of accepted principles from clinicians and survey researchers. Stresses the use of a scientific orientation to the understanding of the intellectual, motor, and emotional dimensions of the interview. A good list of criteria for evaluation is given on pp. 171–172.

ORGANIZATIONAL RESEARCH

CHAPPLE, E. D. Quantitative analysis of complex organizational systems. *Human Organizations* 21 (1962): 67–87.

Chapple imaginatively suggests that the functioning of a complex organizational system may be analyzed in terms of a generalization of his study of formal properties of dyadic communication. The variables include who is acting, who is silent, who interrupts, who initiates action after a mutual silence, and who dominates (continues talking after an interruption).

ROETHLISBERGER, F. J., AND W. J. DICKSON. *Management and the worker*. Cambridge, Mass.: Harvard University Press, 1946.

This classic study of workers' attitudes exploded the use of the nondirective interview for industrial organizational research and for employee counseling. Stressed that the manifest content of employees' interviews was misleading unless underlying latent feelings were understood. The conclusion was that the informal social organization was far more determinate of morale and productivity than was the rational, formal organization of the work and the work group.

WHYTE, W. F. Interviewing for organizational research. *Human Organization*, 12; 2 (1953): 15–22.

An experienced social scientist suggests guidelines for the use of the interview in organizational research.

OPINION SURVEYS

CANNELL, C. F., AND R. L. KAHN. Interviewing. In G. Lindzey and
E. Aronson, Eds. *The handbook of social psychology.* 2nd ed. Vol.
2. Reading, Mass.: Addison-Wesley, 1968. Pp. 526–595.
  A review of current opinions in the field and research on the use
  of the information-gathering interview for opinion surveying and
  other social-psychological research. Defines the measurement
  problems of the interview: validity, reliability, and precision.
  Suggests the conditions for successful interviewing: accessibility
  of respondent, respondent understanding, and respondent motivation, stressing especially the motivational model of interviewing as
  a social process. Reviews empirical findings related to the conditions for successful interviewing, and for the selection and training of interviewers.

GORDEN, R. L. *Interviewing strategy, techniques, and tactics.* Home-
wood, Ill.: Dorsey Press, 1969.
  Intended for planners and supervisors of interviewing and questionnaire research, with some sections relevant to the research
  interviewer and the professional who does occasional interviewing.
  Extended treatment of the rationale of the interview. Some good
  suggestions on interviewing techniques, arrangement of the interviewing schedule, and how to train interviewers.

HYMAN, H. H., W. J. COBB, J. J. FELDMAN, C. W. HART, AND
C. H. STEMBER. *Interviewing in social research.* Chicago: University
of Chicago Press, 1954.
  A thoughtful and thorough examination of the effects of the
  sources of error in the survey research interview. Sources studied
  were the interviewer, the interviewee, and the specific situation.

KAHN, R. L., AND C. F. CANNELL. *The dynamics of interviewing:
Theory, technique and cases.* New York: John Wiley, 1957.
  The authors are survey researchers writing a book for all types of
  interviewing. First is a compilation of several theories—especially
  stressing Rogers and Lewin. Chapter 3 deals in detail with how to
  start an interview to motivate the respondent. Chapter 4 shows
  how to detail the content objectives.

PAYNE, S. L. *The art of asking questions.* Princeton, N.J.: Princeton
University Press, 1951.

Aimed at the question writer for survey research. Payne makes many excellent observations about the semantics of question wording. His suggestions are relevant to all types of interviewing. The book ends with a potent, succinct check list of 100 considerations for wording questions.

RICHARDSON, S. A., B. S. DOHRENWIND, AND D. KLEIN. *Interviewing, its forms and functions.* New York: Basic Books, 1965.

See comments below, p. 188. This book for survey research purposes is as empirically rigorous as Hyman et al. (1954), and has suggested frameworks for understanding the interview which are uncluttered with tangential theory.

CHAPTER 6

BOLSTER, B. I., AND B. M. SPRINGBETT. The reaction of interviewers to favorable and unfavorable information. *Journal of Applied Psychology*, 45 (1961): 97–103.

Programmatic research on the decision-making aspects of interviewing is being conducted at McGill University. These studies investigate the judgmental process in interviewers.

This study found a primacy effect, in that early information was weighted more than later information in terms of final decisions about an employment candidate. Negative information was given more weight than positive information, so that it was easier to induce a shift from a favorable impression to a negative one than vice versa. More weight is also given to any data at any time in the interview that contradict the general set (positive or negative) of the interviewer.

LEVY, H. *Psychological interpretation.* New York: Holt, Rinehart & Winston, 1963.

A logical and procedural analysis of the process of interpretation in clinical psychology. Posits the intellectual steps in making interpretations diagnostically and therapeutically. The subtleties of abstraction from observed data are enormous.

SUNDBERG, D., AND L. E. TYLER. *Clinical psychology: An introduction to research and practice.* New York: Appleton-Century-Crofts, 1962.

Chapter 8, pp. 197–224, depicts the complex process of making inferences. A briefer explanation of Levy's (1963) material.

CHAPTER 7

DAVITZ, J. R. *The language of emotion.* New York: Academic Press, 1969.

Continuing his extended research in emotional expression in language, Davitz presents a helpful dictionary of fifty terms most commonly used to express a variety of feelings. Fifty subjects completed a check list of over 500 entries to help operationalize each term. A dictionary in Chapter 2 gives the definitions and related descriptive states, including the degree of agreement among the respondents.

Are there underlying continua in words used to express feelings? A factor analysis of the 215 items used most in defining the above dictionary definitions yielded three clusters: (1) positive—activation, moving toward, comfort, enhancement; (2) negative type a—hypoactivation, moving away, discomfort, incompetence, dissatisfaction; and (3) negative type b—hyperactivation, moving against, tension, inadequacy. In each cluster, the dimensions of activation, relatedness, hedonic tone, and competence are present.

HOLSTI, O. R. *Content analysis for the social sciences and humanities.* Reading, Mass.: Addison-Wesley, 1969.

A useful compendium of design, procedures, and reliability and validity questions in the use of content analysis of documents.

WIENER, M., AND A. MEHRABIAN. *Language within language: Immediacy, a channel in verbal communication.* New York: Appleton-Century-Crofts, 1968.

Programmatic research on the immediacy concept has shown it to be a rich avenue to data about emotions and attitudes, Especially helpful are the criteria for scoring non-immediacy in Chapter 4. The authors have found nonverbal behaviors also of much significance in measuring the degrees of immediacy with which people communicate.

CHAPTER 8

VERBAL CONDITIONING OF SUBJECTS' RESPONSES—THEORY

How much interview behavior can be altered unknowingly by deliberate, selective reinforcement of desired utterances by the interviewer? From the extensive findings in learning studies comes the highly significant finding that preselected categories of words or statements can be differentially increased over a baseline rate by the simple technique of experimenter or interviewer reinforcement with various verbal and nonverbal cues.

BANDURA, A. Psychotherapy as a learning process. *Psychological Bulletin*, 58 (1961): 143–159.

Introduces operant learning concepts to therapy interactions.

VERBAL CONDITIONING—LITERATURE SURVEYS

Several comprehensive surveys of findings in the experimental laboratory are now available.

GREENSPOON, J. Verbal conditioning and clinical psychology. In A. J. Bachrach, Ed., *Experimental foundations of clinical psychology*. New York: Basic Books, 1962. Pp. 510–533.

KRASNER, L. Studies of the conditioning of verbal behavior. *Psychological Bulletin*, 55 (1958): 148–170.

SALZINGER, K. Experimental manipulation of verbal behavior: A review. *Journal of General Psychology*, 61 (1959): 65–94.

VERBAL CONDITIONING—EXAMPLES OF STUDIES

BEIER, E. G. *The silent language of psychotherapy*. Chicago: Aldine, 1966.

Beier applies learning therapy to the development of nonverbal behavior patterns. He believes that subtle nonverbal cues are learned in infancy and serve to protect the individual from undue anxiety, by constricting the other person's responses. Hence nonverbal patterns function as unconsciously motivated behavior. The resulting constriction of information flow is the basis for malfunctions in communication.

FERGUSON, D. C., AND A. H. BUSS. Operant conditioning of hostile verbs in relation to experimenter and subject characteristics. *Journal of Consulting Psychology*, 24 (1960): 324–327.

Subjects in this experiment were exposed to an aggressive and a neutral interviewer, to test for different amounts of operant conditioning related to hostile verbs. Subjects exposed to the aggressive interviewer did show an increase in use of hostile verbs, but less of an increase than the subjects exposed to the neutral interviewer.

HILDUM, D. C., AND R. W. BROWN. Verbal reinforcement and interviewer bias. *Journal of Abnormal and Social Psychology*, 53 (1956): 108–111.

This well-designed study, conducted by telephone interviewing, found that the lingual reinforcer "good" successfully conditioned, while the utterance "um-hum" did not.

MOOS, R. H. The retention and generalization of operant conditioning effects in an interview situation. *Journal of Abnormal and Social Psychology*, 66 (1963): 52–58.

Head nods and "umm-hmm" were effective in increasing interviewee's utterance of statements of feelings of independence and affection. While this effect lasted with the same interviewer 24 hours later, without further ER reinforcements, the effect did not generalize to a similar stimulus situation that was slightly changed.

MURRAY, E. J. Verbal reinforcement in psychotherapy. *Journal of Consulting and Clinical Psychology*, 32 (1968): 243–246.

Using films of actual therapist behavior, Murray has clearly shown the operation of reinforcement. He began his interest in this question with a film of Rogers doing nondirective therapy, about which Rogers had claimed that the interviewer was not exerting behavioral control over the interviewee. Murray found evidence to the contrary.

SALZINGER, K., AND S. PISONI. Reinforcement of verbal affect responses of normal subjects during the interview. *Journal of Abnormal and Social Psychology*, 60 (1960): 127–130.

Following standard experimental procedures, this study showed that self-referrant affective statements could be conditioned. It also suggested that there may be a threshold below which conditioning does not occur, so the ER has to cue EE at a rate above a lower limit.

WEISS, R. L., L. KRASNER, AND L. P. ULLMAN. On the relationship between hypnotizability and response to verbal operant conditioning. *Psychological Reports*, 6 (1960): 59–60.

This study found that more suggestible subjects were more easily conditioned by the standard procedures.

THE FORM OF THE QUESTION AND
ITS EFFECTS ON THE RESPONSE

KAHN, R. L., AND C. F. CANNELL. *The dynamics of interviewing: Theory, technique and cases.* New York: John Wiley, 1957.

Chapter 8 explores the process of probing, suggesting the use of "controlled nondirective" techniques. In Chapter 9, three criteria for the effectiveness of probing are proposed: acceptance, validity, and relevance to the purpose of the interview. Examples of how to apply these criteria are given.

KINSEY, A. C., W. B. POMEROY, AND C. E. MARTIN. *Sexual behavior in the human male.* Philadelphia, Penn.: W. B. Saunders, 1948.

The pioneering work in the use of the interview to get highly personal information in a large scale opinion survey. Leading questions were deliberately used to generate more quantity and validity of responses.

RICHARDSON, S. A., B. S. DOHRENWIND, AND D. KLEIN. *Interviewing, its forms and functions.* New York: Basic Books, 1965.

In Chapters 6 and 7, the authors exhaustively examine issues and available research findings on the matter of the impact of the form of a question on EE's responses.

Assumptions about the undesirability of directiveness in ER are examined. Stressing the quality of the EE response as the key issue, and the avoidance of ER bias as crucial, the authors explode the myth that the nondirective interview universally generates more valid responses and freer EE verbal expression. Kinsey (1948) found that directiveness produced more valid responses when EE could be expected to be evasive. While one might assume that degree of directiveness might apply to an interview as a whole, the authors observe that a single interview usually has moments of varying degrees. Another assumption about directiveness is that it is aversive to EE: Kinsey (1948) showed otherwise. Another assumption about nondirectiveness needs examination: that it builds better rapport. For some subjects, nondirectiveness might increase ambiguity for them, and increase their anxiety.

Studies of open and closed questions show that the expected long versus short answers do, in fact, occur in a ratio of about 3:1. It may not always be functional to begin an interview with open questions, if EE is doubtful about the specific topic of interest.

A general assumption about leading questions—which imply the answer expected—is that they should not be used. While a question may be stated without an overt or implied ER expectation about EE's specific answer, any question has a premise or assumption about EE having had the experience of interest. In personal history interviews, premises must be derived from prior data about EE. Premises formed accurately on prior data from EE are not the improper leading question proscribed by interviewing writers. A study of experienced and inexperienced interviewers showed that experienced ERs used leading closed questions 33 percent of the time, a figure much higher than expected. Further, the rated skill level of the experienced interviewers was unrelated to their frequency of use of leading questions. By checking the validity of information obtained by the leading questions, it was found that the responses were equally as valid as the answers to all other types of questions. ER should be aware, however, of conditions in EE which prognosticate invalid answers: if EE is afraid to disagree, if EE is eager to please the ER, or if EE is bored and impatient to finish.

LINGUISTIC AND PARALINGUISTIC EFFECTS

PITTENGER, R. E., C. F. HOCKETT, AND J. J. DANEHY. *The first five minutes.* Ithaca, N.Y.: Martineau, 1960.

After their microscopic investigation of the interview, the authors make several suggestions for evaluating ER-EE interactions in an interview.

EE may hide ambiguities by using a second- or third-person pronoun. Likewise, his use of deictics (this, that, there, now, then) may confuse the immediate with the remote.

When EE stops in the middle of a statement and rephrases it, ER may validly guess the finish to the incompleted first beginning. This gives data on stress areas.

Watch for increases or decreases in smoothness of delivery. The typical conversational speech is not very smooth. After gauging the individual EE's norm for smoothness, watch for increases, which may be rehearsal units. The rehearsal units may cover for indecisiveness. Rougher delivery may also indicate milder indecisiveness.

Control may be exerted by variations of volume, register, tempo, and voice. For example, the "road hog" speeds up if he thinks he may be interrupted.

INDEX

71 72 73 74   7 6 5 4 3 2 1